BRITAIN'S COASTLINE

Jerome Monahan

MYRIAD
LONDON

First published in 2007
by Myriad Books Limited,
35 Bishopsthorpe Road,
London SE26 4PA

ISBN 1 84746 013 5
EAN 978 1 84746 013 4

Designed by Jerry Goldie
Graphic Design
Printed in China

www.myriadbooks.com

Title page: South Stack
lighthouse, Holy Island,
Anglesey; this page, the Seven
Sisters from Cuckmere Haven;
opposite, view from Eigg towards
Rhum

Contents

South-East England

England's south-east coast features dockyards, coastal forts and castles – testament to a rich past bound up with the nation's frequent need to defend itself. In the 19th century its fishing villages were transformed into popular seaside resorts and became a magnet for ordinary Londoners. Today much of the south coast is still under siege, this time from the elements and rising sea levels, but this has often created beautiful beaches and spectacular cliffs that have long captured the imagination of artists and poets.

Historic dockyard Chatham *above*

The small Kentish town of Chatham is inseparable from Britain's power as a seagoing nation. Located on the Medway, near where the river joins the Thames, its first docks were established in the reign of Henry VIII and the town continued to be an important naval base until 1984. One of the most famous of the 400-plus Royal Naval vessels built in Chatham's dockyards was Nelson's last ship, *HMS Victory*, constructed between 1759-1765. And it was to Chatham that the young Nelson came in 1771, aged 12, to take up his first post as a midshipman. The photograph is of the No 3 Covered Slip built in 1838. It is one of five dry docks that have survived to this day. The decision to shelter the slipways was taken in order to preserve the vessels from the effects of the weather. In its day No 3 Slip was one of the largest timber-span structures in the world. The working dockyard closed in 1984 but its magnificent Georgian buildings have been transformed into a splendid museum charting Britain's maritime past and its history of shipbuilding.

Rochester Castle

left and below

The town of Rochester owes its development to its position at the mouth of the Medway where it joins the Thames. It is here that the Roman-built Watling Street that links London, Canterbury and Dover crosses the Medway. Its first castle was built in the reign of William I and was one of the earliest English castles to be built of stone. The imposing keep with its 113ft tower constructed from Kentish ragstone was constructed in the ninety-year period from 1127 when the castle was the responsibility of the Archbishops of Canterbury. It has endured a number of sieges over the centuries including one commanded by King John in 1215 during which the southern part of the keep suffered significant damage. Rochester Castle is now owned and maintained by English Heritage.

Isle of Sheppey *left*

It was only in 2006 that the Isle of Sheppey, in the Thames estuary, acquired a permanent dual carriageway road link with mainland Kent. Previously, it had to depend on the Kingsferry Swingbridge built in 1959 which carried both road and rail traffic and which had to be raised periodically to allow ships using the Swale channel to pass. The eastern end of the island is mainly agricultural with a scattering of small villages; at the western end modern container shipping utilises the deep water berths at Sheerness, one of the main ports for the import of cars into the UK.

Whitstable *left* and Herne Bay *right*

Oysters remain central to the identity of Whitstable on the north Kent coast. Now a magnet for artists, Whitstable is enjoying something of a boom. This follows a period of neglect since its heyday in the 19th century when it was a popular seaside resort and boasted a thriving harbour (built 1832), a boatbuilding industry and fishing fleet. The oyster season lasts from September to April and each July the town holds an Oyster Festival. Neighbouring Herne Bay is another seaside resort enjoying a revival having recently secured a European Blue Flag in recognition of its clean beach. Herne Bay has wonderful late Victorian seaside architecture; its glorious bandstand has recently been restored and its brightly-coloured beach huts command eyewatering prices.

Faversham *above and left*

Faversham has a long history dating back to Roman times. On its creek (left), leading onto the Swale, it had access to the open sea and its harbour became central to its economic success. From the 11th century it boasted a considerable abbey nearby, though it was demolished following the Reformation. In the 17th century it was the key port in England involved in the wool trade. In the 18th century Faversham became associated with the manufacture of gunpowder. In 1916 the explosion at the Uplees gunpowder mill killed 109 people and was heard across the Thames estuary at Southend. As London's population grew in the 19th century so did Faversham's importance to the capital as a centre of the manufacture of the famous yellow London stock bricks. Today, one of Faversham's remaining industries is brewing; founded in Faversham in 1698, the independent Kentish brewery Shepherd Neame still makes traditional Kentish ales. This family business is based in the centre of Faversham and owns many splendid pubs.

Margate *above*

A night-time view of the seafront at Margate shows off its bright lights reflected in the tide-damp sands that form the North Kent coast resort's major attraction. Its extensive beaches have been drawing visitors since the late 18th century, making this one of Britain's earliest seaside resorts. Its name is thought to derive from an early term for a cliff gap where pools of water suitable for bathing can be found. In the middle ages it was one of the "limbs" of the Cinque Port of Dover, enjoying privileges alongside the responsibility of providing ships capable of defending the country at time of war. The painter JMW Turner (1775-1881) loved Margate – the quality of the light over the sea drew him back time and time again. There are now plans by Kent County Council to establish a new gallery called Turner Contemporary, an important element in the regeneration of Margate and east Kent.

Rochester *below*

The Medway town is proud of its associations with Charles Dickens who lived nearby at Gads Hill Place, Higham. Every year two festivals celebrate this link – the Summer Dickens Festival in June and the Dickensian Christmas Festival in December. Descriptions of Rochester appear in *The Pickwick Papers* and the town is the inspiration for "Cloisterham" in *The Mystery of Edwin Drood*. The imposing Restoration House in Crow Lane was where, in 1660, Charles II stayed on his royal progress back to London when he claimed the crown and the monarchy was restored after the rule of Oliver Cromwell. By the mid 19th century the house had fallen into disrepair and its dilapidated state and sinister appearance was the inspiration for Satis House, the home of Miss Havisham, in *Great Expectations*. Restoration House is open to the public during the summer.

Rochester is also home to England's second oldest cathedral and the town centre boasts a clutch of beautiful buildings including the Guildhall.

Broadstairs *right*

Nicknamed the "jewel in Thanet's Crown", Broadstairs benefits from no less than seven local sandy beaches; the view is of Viking Bay – so-named because it is thought that Hengist and Horsa landed here in 449 at the head of a Jute army that would go on to help create the Kingdom of Kent. Broadstairs has strong Charles Dickens associations. He was a frequent visitor and wrote *David Copperfield* here, basing the character of Betsy Trotwood on local resident Mary Pearson Strong, whose former home is now a museum dedicated to the author.

Deal Castle *left*

Deal is thought to be the site of Julius Caesar's landing in 55BC. One of its most prominent sites is its Tudor castle built in the reign of Henry VIII; it is one of a series of "Device Forts" constructed as a coastal defence following an alliance between France and Spain in 1538.

Dover *right and below*

Dover was the most prominent of the five Cinque Ports created in the mid 11th century during the reign of Edward the Confessor and charged with "ship service" – providing naval vessels and men needed to protect England in exchange for many civic privileges including running their own judicial affairs. The port (right) of today is one of the busiest in the UK handling a huge amount of cross-Channel traffic, including 18m passengers. The history of Dover Castle (below) dates back to pre-Roman times as proved by the remains of earthworks discovered by archaeologists. The current fortress was mainly laid out in Henry II's reign but underwent significant rebuilding during the Napoleonic Wars including the construction of underground tunnels designed to house a substantial garrison. In the Second World War the tunnels were used as air-raid shelters.

White Cliffs *right*

For the British, the White Cliffs of Dover are full of symbolism, defining the country's independence from Continental Europe and forming a natural bastion at times of threatened invasion. Created over a period of 80 million years following the last Ice Age, they have been designated a Site of Special Scientific Interest thanks to the specific plant, animal and insect life that thrives on the cliffsides and tops. The cliffs provide a good roosting place for a variety of birds including black-tipped gulls, fulmars and kittiwakes and are also a regular stopping-off point for migrating birds.

East Wear Bay *below*

Situated to the east of Folkestone, East Wear Bay was notorious for many centuries as a key landing place for contraband.

Dungeness

Dungeness is an other-worldly spot on the Kent coast where extensive shingle deposits (the most substantial in Europe) have created an extraordinary landscape. Apart from the two nearby nuclear power stations, the only other major buildings in the area are two lighthouses. The 1901 lighthouse (above) is now a tourist attraction. Prospect Cottage (right) was owned by the artist and film director Derek Jarman who created a much-visited garden using local hardy plants, pebbles and beachcombing "finds". There is a 2,500-acre RSPB nature reserve at Dungeness. This beautiful spot can be reached by the miniature steam trains of the Romney, Hythe and Dymchurch Railway.

Hythe Royal Military Canal *right*

The Royal Military Canal stretches for 28 miles and was built as a defence against Napoleon. The canal is in two sections – the longest from Hythe in Kent which ends at Iden Lock in East Sussex. After the Battle of Waterloo, the canal acquired a second function as a bulwark against local smugglers. It is now used by the Environment Agency to manage water levels across much of Romney Marsh and is vital to the area's flood protection.

Camber Sands *above*

The only sand dune system in East Sussex is to be found at Camber and it provides an important habitat for many species of animals and plants. The grasses are rumoured to have arrived here as a lost cargo of seeds destined for South America. Camber Sands has seen many wrecks and has been used as a location for a number of films, including the Dunkirk evacuation beaches in *The Battle Of Britain* and the Sahara in *Carry On – Follow That Camel*. It is popular with fashion photographers.

13

Hastings

Hastings was one of the original Cinque Ports. Its position as a centre of maritime power was undermined in the 13th century due to a combination of storms that washed the town into the sea and repeated raids by the French. Hastings lost out to other coastal towns due to its lack of a harbour. Its boats are still forced to moor on the beach (above). An attempt in the late 19th century to build a harbour ran into financial problems and the construction work that had been completed was then blown up in the Second World War as a defensive measure. Hastings is famous for its curiously shaped Victorian "net shops" (left) used by the town's fishermen for storage. The shops were tall and narrow to avoid ground taxes. There is currently a restoration programme underway to preserve and restore these unique beach landmarks.

Hastings Pier *above*

The coastal view to the west takes in Hastings and its 19th-century pier. The pier has recently been condemned as unsafe, due to parts of the structure falling onto the beach below. Over the centuries one of the town's most prominent local enterprises involved the smuggling of contraband. Today, tourism is the area's principle business. Hastings has long been known as a retreat for artists including the pre-Raphaelite painters Dante Gabriel Rossetti and William Holman Hunt.

Bexhill-on-Sea *right*

In 722 King Offa granted *Bexelei* (later to become Bexhill-on-Sea) the right to found a church. Its recent history is closely associated with the De La Warrs who married into the Sackville family, the principal local landowners from the 16th-19th centuries. The family began the extensive construction work that helped Bexhill-on-Sea become a fashionable resort. The 9th

Earl championed one of the town's most famous buildings, the De La Warr Pavilion which was opened in 1935. This magnificent Modernist building, with its gallery, cinema and restaurants, has now been completely restored and re-opened to the public in 2005.

Eastbourne *right*

Eastbourne, on the East Sussex coast, is the most easterly point of the extensive chalk escarpment of the South Downs. Although the town has a long history with evidence of prehistoric and Roman occupation, it remained a mere scattering of settlements until the 19th century when the two principal local landowners, the Duke of Devonshire and John Davies-Gilbert, decided to develop a resort to rival other fashionable seaside towns. They commissioned the architect Henry Currey to lay out an entire new town. Originally intended as a place "built by gentlemen for gentlemen", it suffered badly in bombing raids during the Second World War and many of the Victorian splendours that survived were lost in the post-war years due to insensitive planning decisions. The seafront however retains its elegance and no shops are allowed on the front. Eastbourne hits the headlines every year when it stages a major women's tennis championship treated by competitors as a warm-up before Wimbledon.

Seaford *left*

Rockpools and cliffs adjacent to the modest resort town of Seaford. The Martello Tower, situated at the eastern end of the seafront, was built at the westernmost end of the defences constructed during the Napoleonic Wars. Today the tower is a museum telling the story of the town going back to the days of its prominence as part of the network of Cinque Ports and "limbs" set up to defend the coast in medieval times. Close by is the Belle Tout Lighthouse, a famous landmark on the cliffs built in 1832. Now a private house, the entire structure had to be moved back from the cliff's edge to prevent it tumbling into the sea.

Beachy Head *above and left*

The chalk headland at Beachy Head rises to over 535ft (163m) above sea level and is one of the most spectacular spots on the south coast. At this point the undulating cliffs form themselves into a number of headlands known as the Seven Sisters. This line of cliffs is receding at approximately 2-3ins per year due to coastal erosion; major rock falls often occur after heavy rain or rough seas. During the latter part of the 17th century the sea just off Beachy Head saw two naval engagements; the second in 1690 resulted in defeat for a combined English and Dutch fleet at the hands of the French – in a conflict known as The War of the Grand Alliance (1699-1697). Beachy Head has also been hazardous for shipping in more peaceful times and the 1902 Matthews Lighthouse is the third to have been built on or near the cliffs to safeguard shipping. Its light is visible up to 25 nautical miles out to sea.

Brighton

Brighton is one of the largest and best known of Britain's many seaside resorts. Once it was merely a fishing village called Brighthelmston, but its fortunes waxed with the increasing popularity of sea bathing (and sea water drinking) as a cure for all manner of ills – an approach encouraged by a Dr Richard Russell of Lewes in the 1740s and 1750s. Brighton has long been a fashionable destination – a pattern established when the Prince Regent (later George IV) made it a favourite spot in the 1790s. He commissioned Thomas Nash to design the exotic Royal Pavilion, built between 1815 and 1822. Other major Brighton landmarks are its two piers. The West Pier (above) was built in 1866. It has been closed since 1975 awaiting renovation and then suffered significant fire damage in 2004. The town's other pier is the Palace – built in 1891 it attracts over two million visitors every year. Brighton has strong literary and artistic associations; Graham Greene's novel *Brighton Rock* focuses on the town's criminal gangs of the inter-war years.

Hove *right*

Beach huts on the promenade in Hove are much in demand and are rented from the council. They rarely become available and when they do tenancies are decided by lottery. Hove remained separate from nearby Brighton until the mid-19th century. The centre of the modern part of the town is Brunswick Terrace, which has had a number of famous residents including the Austrian leader Prince Metternich who was driven from his country in 1848 – the year of revolutions across Europe.

Worthing *below*

The West Sussex town of Worthing has a colourful history. It was long associated with smuggling and in the late 19th century was a hotbed of agitation against the temperance campaigners. Between 1884 and 1892 there was significant violence as the so-called Skeleton Army – formed in Worthing and made up of toughs recruited by pub and brothel-owners – confronted the Salvation Army disrupting its rallies and beating up its members. Gentler pastimes prevail today as Worthing is the base of the English Bowling Association. Worthing Pier (below) was opened in 1862.

West Wittering *above*

This small town has survived much of the rapid development that blights many coastal towns. This is thanks to local campaigners who worked hard in the 1950s and 60s to preserve the natural beauty of the area. The beach and its surrounding marshland is still managed by a private local conservation charity in combination with English Nature. At low tide over half a mile of sand is exposed.

Bosham *left*

Bosham is two separate settlements. Old Bosham (shown here) was known to the Romans and earns a mention in the Venerable Bede's *Ecclesiastical History of England* since it was from here that St Wilfred launched his campaign to convert the South Saxons to Christianity in the late seventh century. Holy Trinity church is the town's most significant landmark and is considered to be one of the oldest religious buildings in Sussex. The people of Bosham won wide praise in the plague year of 1664 when they kept nearby Chichester – then in strict quarantine – supplied with food.

Selsey *right*

First opened in 1860, the lifeboat station at Selsey is a striking structure along this part of the West Sussex coastline. Selsey's name derives from "seal island" – a reminder that it lies on the narrow Manhood Peninsula, a small island almost cut off from the mainland by the sea. The museum, adjacent to the lifeboat station, charts the history of Selsey and its lifeboats. Erosion and periodic flooding are a continual problem for this area which was once reliant on its fishing industries. Today the town's fortunes are tied up with tourism; the road into the town is busy with holiday traffic during the summer.

Littlehampton *left*

Boats and picturesque stone and wooden buildings line Littlehampton's riverside front. The town has developed on the east bank of the mouth of the river Arun as it flows out into the English Channel. Littlehampton's history dates back to Saxon times, although there have been Roman finds within the confines of the modern town. Its name derives from the medieval sailor's practice of calling the settlement here "Little Hampton" in order to distinguish it from nearby Southampton. Littlehampton gained a reputation as a favourite spot for artists and writers, attracted by its peaceful atmosphere and two beautiful beaches. In particular, Percy Bysshe Shelley and Samuel Taylor Coleridge spent a great deal of time here, as did Lord Byron who often swam in the river. The arrival of the railway in 1863 brought with it holiday crowds and the town still owes its fortunes to seasonal influxes of visitors. Its most famous resident is Anita Roddick who founded the Body Shop, whose headquarters are still in the town.

Langstone and Hayling Island

Langstone is a picturesque village located on the
northern shores of Chichester Harbour. Its waterfront
includes the Old Mill (right), the Royal Oak public
house and some fishermen's cottages, which are a
favourite subject for photographers and painters.
Hayling Island (below) lies off the coast of Hampshire.
Ten miles square, it is shaped like an inverted capital
"T" and is connected to the mainland by a roadbridge.
It is a popular holiday destination and famous among
watersports enthusiasts as being the place where
windsurfing was invented. Its waters are clean and the
foreshore at West Beachlands has European Blue Flag
accreditation. In 1996 the historic oysterbeds on the
north-west coast of Hayling Island were restored by
the local council, creating a wildlife haven. "Hayling"
is a Saxon word meaning "Hegel's People"; before they
settled the Romans left their mark, building at least
one structure on the northern part of the island.

Portsmouth *right*

Portsmouth is a busy city on the Hampshire coast, with a population of about 190,000. Its history and fortunes are intertwined with that of the Royal Navy; it is home to a major dockyard and its economy is reliant on commercial maritime operations. The town's growth began in the 12th century following the building of an Augustinian Priory at Southwick. It became an established port during the reign of King John (1199-1216) and it was frequently the launchpad for attacks on France. The first fortifications in Portsmouth were built by Henry V. The Round Tower (right) is a later addition to the town's defences – built in stone by order of Henry VIII. One of the town's most famous attractions dates from his reign – the flagship the *Mary Rose* which sank in the harbour in 1545 and was salvaged in 1984. Many historic ships can be seen by ferry passengers as they leave Portsmouth harbour.

HMS Warrior *above* and The Spinnaker Tower *right*

Portsmouth is the site of the first dry dock in Britain, built during the reign of Henry VIII. The Historic Dockyard is now a major tourist attraction – home to Nelson's flagship *HMS Victory* and *HMS Warrior*, the world's first iron-hulled battleship built in 1860. When she was built, this ship made every other military vessel in the world obsolete. The dockyard gives a unique insight into the life of royal naval seamen over 150 years ago.

The splendid Spinnaker Tower, built between 2003-5, was designed to reflect the city's maritime history. At 558ft (170m) high it is two and a half times the height of Nelson's Column, making it the tallest accessible structure in Britain outside London. The tower's twin concrete legs meet halfway up forming a single column from which steel sails are mounted; an observation deck at the top provides visitors with a panoramic view of the harbour and city.

Cowes

Cowes is the Isle of Wight's main port. It is a natural harbour and renowned for sailing. It is home to Royal Yacht Squadron – one of the most prestigious yacht clubs in the world. Since 1854 this has operated from its base in Cowes Castle (left) a former Tudor stronghold. It is also here during the first week of August that the world's oldest regatta is held. Cowes' origins are humble. It was once a fishing community sandwiched between two forts built during Henry VIII's reign. The "cows" from which the town derives its name are actually two sandbanks that lie offshore. However, its reputation for shipbuilding took off and the patronage of George IV, a keen sailor, helped to establish the town's position as the yachting capital of the world.

The Needles

The row of stacks known as The Needles are one of the best-known and most spectacular sights along the south coast. They take their name from a sharp stone called Lot's Wife that used to stand there until it fell down in a storm in 1764. There has long been a military presence on the cliffs near the Needles with batteries of cannon placed there to protect the western approach to the Solent – the stretch of water between the Isle of Wight and the mainland coast. The Needles Lighthouse was constructed in 1855 at sea-level; it replaced the 1786 cliff-top lighthouse which was often shrouded in cloud.

Alum Bay *right*

Adjacent to The Needles, Alum Bay is another part of this coast affected by severe erosion. Climbing the attractive sandstone cliffs was once a popular pastime but the crumbling state of the rocks today makes this hazardous. The Bay's famous coloured sand is collected when there are cliff falls and sold in glass containers. Alum Bay once had a pier on the beach but it was damaged in 1927 and not repaired. During the summer season a popular chairlift takes tourists down to the beach below.

Compton Bay *above*

A view to the north-west takes in the sweep of the Isle of Wight's south coast with Compton Bay in the foreground and the cliffs of Freshwater Bay glittering in the distance. This side of the island is less developed than the east and north coasts, mainly because it is subject to the prevailing south-west winds and is experiencing considerable erosion.

Freshwater Bay *right*

The dramatic cliffs at Freshwater Bay are subject to considerable erosion; a local landmark, the Arch Rock, collapsed in 1994. A short way inland the village of Freshwater attracts visitors because of its association with Alfred Lord Tennyson who lived at Farringford House for over 40 years. It is considered one of the finest examples of Victorian architecture on the island after Osborne House – Queen Victoria's retreat. Another famous "local" was the 19th century photographer Julia Margaret Cameron. Her house, Dimbola Lodge, is now a museum.

Sandown *above*

Crowds gather on the sandy expanse of beach that runs around Sandown Bay on the south-east coast of the island. It shares the Bay with Shanklin and Yaverland while to the north are Culver Cliffs – famous for the prehistoric remains they deposit onto the beach with every slippage and rock fall. Sandown is home to the Dinosaur Isle museum – the UK's first purpose-built dinosaur museum, which has been designed in the shape of a giant pterodactyl. The museum has many exciting exhibits including animated dinosaurs and lifesize reconstructions.

Yarmouth *right*

Yarmouth is a port with a deepwater harbour on the west coast of the island. The town contains a famous monument to Admiral Sir Robert Holmes who, in a naval action against the French, captured an incomplete statue of the then French king Louis XIV. The sculptor was forced to complete it in Holmes' likeness. It can now be seen in St James' Church.

Port Solent *above*

The marina at Port Solent was just one of several proposed schemes for the reclaimed land at Northarbour, within Portsmouth Harbour. Alternative schemes included a Commonwealth Games venue and a huge conference centre. The marina was first proposed in 1981 but it took several years of discussion before a final scheme was approved. As well as offering hundreds of berths, Port Solent has a Boardwalk with a variety of shops, restaurants and a health centre.

Buckler's Hard *right*

The idyllic village of Buckler's Hard on the river Beaulieu owes its existence to the second Duke of Montagu who aimed to create a port for the import of West Indian sugar. The idea came to nothing but a considerable shipbuilding industry grew up instead. It was here that many of the ships that fought at Trafalgar were built by master shipwright Henry Adams and his sons. The area also played a part in later victories. The famous Mulberry Harbours were built here. Following the D-Day landings in Normandy in June 1944 their role was to keep the allied forces supplied. The river Beaulieu is a nature reserve and home to many rare bird species.

South-West England

The towns and villages of south-west England may seem benign today but most have darker histories, featuring the worst of human activities – war, smuggling and wrecking. Grim times surrendered eventually to respectability thanks in large part to the railways that opened up the coast to Victorian holidaymakers, making tourist spots and artists' colonies of places previously known only for their poverty, isolation and toughness of life. Today the tremendous legacy of this coast is there for everyone to experience, coupled with scenery which ranges from the grandeur of Dorset's Jurassic coast to the beautiful bays of Cornwall.

Lymington *above*

The pretty town of Lymington is a port on the Solent in Hampshire. It has a sizeable population of around 40,000, swollen in the summer thanks to its fame as a yachting centre and the attractions of the nearby New Forest. Its origins are Saxon and go back as far as the sixth century when a settlement was created here called *Limen* (meaning either an "elm-lined" or "marshy" river) and the word "tun" meaning a farm or hamlet. The town has had a turbulent past, suffering destruction twice in the 100 Years War at the hands of the French. In the middle ages Lymington was known for its salt production, using coal fires, but this died out finally in the 1860s when natural salt was found in Cheshire. Smuggling was also an important aspect of the town's economy.

Bournemouth *below*

Adjacent to Poole, Bournemouth, with its glorious sandy beach, owes its early development to the efforts of Lewis Tregonwell – a retired army officer who visited the area in 1810 and decided to settle there, building a fashionable home and a pine walk to the beach. It was his planting of pine trees in "the chines" (the deep valleys that characterise the area) that attracted visitors to the area. It was thought that the scent of the pine needles could relieve the symptoms of tuberculosis. By the early years of the 20th century Bournemouth had become a fashionable town with a population of over 50,000, and its position as a holiday and retirement destination was established. The current pier (below) designed by Eugenius Birch was built in 1880. He is also credited with designing the West Pier in Brighton.

Poole *left and above*

The Sandbanks – a small spit of land that has formed across the harbour mouth of the popular seaside town Poole – has some of the highest land values in the UK. In the middle ages Poole enjoyed boom times as a key staging-post in the export of wool. It was burnt down in a Spanish raid in 1405 – provoked in part by raids carried out on their shipping by local pirate Harry Paye. For the last 150 years the town's fortunes have been more closely associated with holidaymakers and those seeking a comfortable retirement.

Chesil Beach *right*

Chesil Beach, or Chesil Bank, is one of the greatest examples of the geological formation known as a "tombolo" in the world. This is a spit of land formed by longshore drift that has over time completely sealed in a section of coast, creating a number of lagoons. It is 17 miles long and has been built up by the steady deposition of flint and chert pebbles – the bulkiest towards Portland and the smaller ones at the Abbotsbury end of the bar. Some local fishermen say they can tell exactly where a Chesil Bank pebble comes from according to its size. One major beneficiary of Chesil Beach is the village of Chiswell, which lies below sea level and is protected by it from storms and high tides.

Old Harry *below*

Old Harry is a chalk stack that marks the point where the Purbeck Hills fall into the sea on the Dorset coast below Ballard Down. Old Harry is about 200 years old. "He" used to be permanently accompanied by a smaller stump called Old Harry's Wife, but "she" collapsed in the 1950s and only reappears during the low spring tides. The name "Old Harry" refers to the devil who is said to have rested on the rock.

Weymouth *right*

Weymouth is situated on a sheltered bay at the mouth of the Wey on the Dorset coast and is today a major tourist destination and a centre for yachting. King George III liked Weymouth and made it fashionable; he bought a house in the town and much of the seafront architecture is Georgian. The king is said to have been offended by a chalk carving of a horse, meant to represent him, which the sculptor designed facing inland. Dismayed that his work had generated royal disapproval, the artist killed himself.

Lulworth Cove *right* and Durdle Door *below*

Lulworth Cove is a horseshoe-shaped natural harbour on the Dorset coast, which attracts thousands of visitors each year. The cove is famous for its geology with the "folded strata" that forms it clearly visible. The local environment supports a wide variety of natural species including one unique species of butterfly – the Lulworth Skipper, discovered near the natural arch Durdle Door in 1832.

Lyme Regis *right*

Lyme Regis is one of the best known coastal towns in Dorset. The Cobb which projects out into Lyme Bay and creates a harbour was first mentioned in the reign of Edward III. Lyme's peak period as a port lasted from the 16th to the 18th centuries; until the 1780s it handled more shipping than Liverpool. Lyme Regis has strong literary associations, featuring in Jane Austen's *Northanger Abbey* and *Persuasion,* and John Fowles' *The French Lieutenant's Woman.*

Monmouth Bay *below*

Monmouth Bay, adjacent to Lyme Regis, is famous for its fossils. Here an ammonite is clearly visible in one of the Blue Lias stones which litter the foreshore. Many of the earliest discoveries of dinosaur and other prehistoric reptile remains were made in this area notably those discovered by Mary Anning (1799–1847). She was a poor local widow who earned money by selling fossils which she had collected from the cliffs and foreshore.

Golden Cap *left*

If ever there was a spot to sit and stare then it is on the Golden Cap – the stretch of coast between the towns of Bridport and Lyme Regis. Here the cliffs reach their highest point along the entire south coast of England climbing to 650ft (192m). Along with the rest of the Jurassic Coast, the Golden Cap enjoys World Heritage Site status. The name derives from the golden greensand rock that literally "caps" the tops of the cliffs here. The beaches below the Golden Cap are famous for their fossils but can be hazardous and are subject to rock falls. They are also swamped at high tide and unwary fossil-hunters should always guard against the risk of being caught and stranded.

Budleigh Salterton *above*

Dinghies and other small boats dry in the sun on Budleigh Salterton's pebble foreshore. This picturesque town in East Devon whose name is derived from its early history as an area of salt-pans, is famous for its associations with Sir Walter Raleigh who was born nearby at Hayes Barton. It was here that Sir John Everett Millais chose to set his famous painting of 1871 – *The Boyhood of Raleigh*. Budleigh Salterton is famous for its red cliffs and is a popular holiday resort. Nearby is the river Otter – celebrated in the poetry of Coleridge. Budleigh Salterton is a peaceful and unspoiled town – even its sports are of a gentle sort. The town boasts the largest croquet lawn outside London.

Teignmouth *left*

Teignmouth's trading activities date back to the 13th century and this little port still handles clay, timber and grain. The town is located on the mouth of the Teign estuary and there are two distinct aspects – the seaward side which is a place of elegant promenades and gardens, and the estuary where moored boats create a picturesque scene. The town has suffered in war and was burnt down in 1690 during a French raid. It is also famous for more peaceful pursuits: the poet Keats completed his epic poem *Endymion* here and it is also associated with local resident Charles Babbage (1791-1871), "the father of computing" who devised the programmable computer.

Brixham *below*

Brixham has a reputation as a seafood centre and the fresh fish stalls on the quayside are a popular port of call for visitors. The town earned a reputation for smuggling in the 18th century. In one famous incident contraband was transported in coffins during an outbreak of cholera. Brixham played an important role during the D-Day landings in 1944 when US troops, destined for Utah Beach in Normandy, embarked from the little harbour.

Paignton *above*

Torquay and Brixham both have more sheltered harbours than Paignton. This did not prevent the small town from developing rapidly as a tourist resort when the Torbay and Dartmouth Railway opened to passengers in 1859. One of the town's biggest attractions is Paignton Zoo – one of the largest in Britain. Oldway Mansion, a well-known local landmark modelled on Versailles, was once the home of Isaac Singer, the sewing machine pioneer.

Torquay *above*

Torquay is the best-known of Torbay's "English Riviera" towns. Its history may stretch back over 1,000 years but its current fortunes owe the most to its popularity as a resort in the late 18th and early 19th centuries. It first came to prominence when naval officers stationed there during the Napoleonic Wars spread the word of its pleasant climate and aspect. Torquay is closely associated with crime-writer Agatha Christie, who was born here in 1890. Today there is a specially devised walk that allows visitors to combines sightseeing with a little amateur sleuthing.

Anstey's Cove, Torquay *left*

Anstey's Cove is a small rocky beach nestling between high cliffs and a thickly wooded hillside, near Torquay. It is one of around 20 beaches that punctuate the 22-mile long English Riviera. The cove enjoys a modicum of fame having been celebrated in verse by arguably the worst poet to write in English, Willliam McGonagall. In *Beautiful Torquay* he writes:

> *And as the tourist there in search of beautiful spots doth rove,*
> *Let them not forget to enquire for Anstey's Cove,*
> *And there they will see a beautiful beach of milky white,*
> *And the sight will fill their hearts with delight.*

Dartmouth *below*

Famous for its naval training college, which all officers of the Royal Navy attend, Dartmouth is situated on the banks of the river Dart. Its deep waters have allowed a strategic harbour to be developed. It was from here that Richard the Lionheart's armies set off for the Crusades in the 12th century, and it has also been subject to attack – twice during the 100 Years War against France in the 14th century after which a huge chain was placed across the Dart to prevent such raids. One of the town's most famous sites is the old wharf of Bayard's Cove. Its 18th-century buildings have featured in a number of TV series including the long-running *Onedin Line*.

Start Point *above*

This isolated peninsula projects nearly a mile out into the sea and marks the southern end of Start Bay which runs from here to Dartmouth. This can be a bleak spot and has been the site of many shipwrecks; a lighthouse was built here in 1836. In the summer months, Start Point's isolation and birdlife make it a popular spot for visitors.

Beesands and Slapton *left*

Beesands in Start Bay has had a colourful past but today the settlement is under threat from coastal erosion, exacerbated by spring and autumn storms. To protect the village new sea walls were constructed in 1991, but they are already being undermined, a fate that befell its neighbour Hallsands at the beginning of the 20th century when a gravel bank was dredged for the construction of the dockyard at Devonport and the village was subsequently washed into the sea. The long shingle strand at Slapton was used extensively by US forces to practise amphibious landings in the build-up to D-Day. The local population was evacuated in 1943 to allow the use of live ammunition in these exercises.

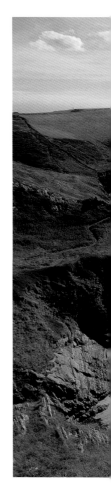

Salcombe *right*

With its natural harbour Salcombe has long been associated with shipbuilding and sailing. In the years between 1796 and 1887, the Salcombe shipyards built three new ships every two years. The mid 19th century was also a boom time for Salcombe's port but the development of steam-driven, steel-hulled craft meant that shipbuilding moved away from places like Salcombe to more industrial centres. The arrival of the railways enabled Salcombe to benefit from the growing tourism to the south-west.

Prawle Point *below*

This is the southernmost point on the Devon coast and is well-known for its varied wildlife and the range of plants found here. A rare bird, the cirl bunting, is known to nest in the area. At particularly low tides the remains of the *Demetrios*, wrecked here in 1992, come into view.

Burgh Island from Bantham Beach *above*

This island off the Devon coast has strong Agatha Christie associations. Its Art Deco hotel provided an inspirational backdrop in several of her stories including the Hercule Poirot novel *Evil Under The Sun*. Famous visitors to the hotel include Churchill, Noel Coward and the Beatles. The island has had a colourful history and was completely cut off during the Second World War for fear that an invading German force might use its causeway to attack the mainland.

Plymouth *above and right*

With its spectacular natural harbour, Plymouth lies at the mouths of two rivers – the Plym and the Tamar. It has been home to two Royal Naval bases and is associated with many of the most famous figures in England's maritime history. In the 16th century the merchants Sir William Hawkins and his son Sir John Hawkins established the grim triangle trade from Plymouth, exchanging manufactured goods for West African slaves and transporting them to the Spanish colonies in Central and South America. Plymouth has seen some famous arrivals and departures. The American Indian princess Pocahontas landed in Plymouth in 1616 and it was from here that the *Mayflower* departed to set up the Plymouth Colony in America in 1620. Its military importance resulted in heavy bombing during the Second World War – in all 1,172 people were killed in air raids. Plymouth is currently undergoing a massive process of urban redevelopment.

Polperro *below*

This pretty fishing village is located on the river Pol, just four miles from Looe. It is now a major tourist destination, with visitors drawn to its attractive harbour and its tightly-packed whitewashed houses. The village has not always been so benign. Significant smuggling operations were carried out in Polperro during the 17th and 18th centuries particularly at times of war with France. The Methodist preacher John Wesley remarked after visiting Polperro in 1762: "An accursed thing among them: well nigh one and all bought or sold uncustomed goods."

Rame Head *above*

This is a popular picnic spot about three miles from Plymouth. The path leading to it passes through bluebell woods and the grounds of Mount Edgcumbe House. The 14th-century chapel dedicated to St Michael is now ruined and is thought to be located on the site of a Celtic hermitage. Rame Head is a great spot for birdspotting; as well as buzzards, kestrels and peregrine falcons, the ultra-rare Dartford Warbler has been sighted.

Fowey *right*

One of Cornwall's oldest and most important ports, Fowey is strongly associated with the trade in china clay and today is known as a yachting centre. It was a key staging post on the "Saints Way" – the pilgrim route through Cornwall linking Ireland and Compostela in northern Spain. Legend has it that Jesus visited Fowey as a child, brought here by Joseph of Arimathea who had tin-trading interests in the town. The town has inspired a number of writers including Daphne du Maurier and Kenneth Grahame.

St Michael's Mount *above*

Linked to the mainland by its regularly submerged causeway, St Michael's Mount deserves to rank among the most spectacular and romantic spots anywhere along the British coast. It has been a priory, fortress, a place of pilgrimage and, since 1659, a private home belonging to the St Aubyn family. It is now one of the National Trust's most visited sites.

Mousehole *below*

Mousehole is pronounced "Mauzl" and is one of Cornwall's most well-known fishing villages with a lovely harbour. In December 1981 the town was engulfed by disaster when the Penlee lifeboat and its eight-man crew were lost. To this day the Christmas lights are turned off on December 19th in commemoration of those that died.

Falmouth *above*

One of Cornwall's gems, Falmouth is a picturesque town, with many seafaring connections. It was from here that a number of successful round-the-world yachting attempts have begun or ended including those of Sir Francis Chichester and Dame Ellen MacArthur. The town is protected by Pendennis Castle, completed in 1540. The castle was one of the last fortified places in England to fall to parliamentary forces during the Civil War. News of victory at the Battle of Trafalgar and Nelson's death came ashore here from the schooner *Pickle*. The town's modern fortunes are linked to the arrival of the railway in 1863 which opened it up to holidaymakers. Falmouth has featured in a number of films including the 1950 version of *Treasure Island*.

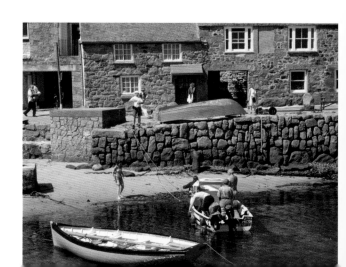

Land's End *above*

This is the most westerly point on mainland Britain. The Longships lighthouse lies within sight of the shore, located on an island of the same name. In Arthurian legend, the halfway point between Land's End and the Isles of Scilly is where the mythical land of Lyonesse was located before the ocean swallowed it up. Land's End is the meeting place of the northern and southern sections of the Cornish coastal footpath.

Minack Theatre

This open-air theatre is built on a granite outcrop near Porthcurno in Cornwall. It owes its existence to Miss Rowena Cade who allowed a group of local actors the chance to perform *The Tempest* on the rocks adjacent to her home, Minack Cottage, in 1930. Every 10 years there is a commemorative performance of *The Tempest*.

Newlyn *above*

Life in Newlyn has traditionally centred on its harbour and fishing fleet. The town was home to William Lovett, one of the leaders of the Chartist Movement which was dedicated to bringing about electoral reform in Britain. It is also known for the Newlyn riots in 1896 caused by the local fishermen – strong sabbatarians all – taking exception to crews from the north of England landing fish on Sunday. In the 1890s the town was adopted by a group of artists, later to be known as the Newlyn School. A staple of their work was everyday life in the village and its surroundings.

St Ives *above and below*

St Ives derives its name from Saint Ia who is said to have arrived here in the fifth century from Ireland. It is an exquisite seaside town bounded by two sandy beaches and provides visitors with experiences far beyond those of the usual seaside resorts thanks to the town's rich artistic heritage. St Ives' fortunes once rested upon its fishing industry. Now it relies on tourism boosted by the presence of no less than two significant art museums including a branch of the Tate (below). The town is associated with Ben Nicholson, Barbara Hepworth and Naum Gabo who all settled here, forming one of the 20th century's most significant artists' colonies anywhere in Britain. It was also the home of Bernard Leach – a key figure in modern art pottery.

Godrevy Point *above*

The name Godrevy comes from the plural of *godref*, which means "hut" or "homestead". Godrevy Island has been the site of many shipwrecks. The Godrevy lighthouse dates from 1857, and was the inspiration for the Modernist novel by Virginia Woolf entitled *To the Lighthouse*. Throughout its first section Mrs Ramsay is constantly thwarted in her desire to visit the lighthouse; poignantly the journey is only made after her death. Godrevy Headland is owned by the National Trust and has a long history of human settlement dating back to the Stone Age. This is an area rich in wildlife. Seals are a common sight and guillemot, razorbill, fulmar and cormorant breed on the cliffs.

Carn Galver mine *left*
One of the many tin and copper mines that lie between St Ives and St Just, Carn Galver ceased operating in 1878. In its heyday it employed 70 miners, but it was never economically viable. The mine is now in the care of the National Trust.

Padstow *right*
The small town of Padstow is located at the mouth of the river Camel. Its history includes the grim activities of local "wreckers", expert in misleading shipping onto the rocks or the "Doom Bar", a notoriously dangerous sandbar in the estuary, often killing those few crew or passengers that made it to shore.

Bedruthan Steps *below*
In spring, pink fields of thrift soften the clifftops of the cliffs overlooking Bedruthan Steps – a set of granite stacks that emerge some 200ft (61m) from the sea. Bedruthan was a legendary giant fabled for using the steps as a causeway.

Bude *below*

The coast near Bude – a small seaside town on the north Cornish coast at the mouth of the river Neet as it flows into Bude Bay – appears deceptively tranquil during a summer sunset. In storms many ships have ended up broken on the reefs that fringe the coast and the local churchyard even contains the figurehead of one of the most famous casualties – the *Bencoolen*, wrecked in 1862.

Lynmouth *right*

The Rising Sun Inn on Mars Hill is one of Lynmouth's most famous attractions. Once a haunt of smugglers, it was here that author RD Blackmore wrote several chapters of *Lorna Doone*. Lynmouth is one of north Devon's most attractive seaside villages, lying on the northern edge of Exmoor at the meeting place of the West and East Lyn rivers. The town has a troubled history. In August 1952 a two-day storm over an already waterlogged Exmoor led to a torrent of debris-carrying water descending on the town. Thirty-four people died, 420 lost their homes and 100 buildings were destroyed.

Lundy *above*

Located off the north Devon coast Lundy is the site of England's only marine nature reserve. For many centuries it was a lawless place – a refuge for pirates who preyed on traffic in the Bristol Channel. It only gained respectability when it was purchased by the Heaven family in the 1830s. In 1969 Lundy became the responsibility of the Landmark Trust. The island is rich in wildlife – particularly seabirds and mammals including the pygmy shrew. Its name derives from the Norse word for a puffin.

Woolacombe *right*

With its golden sands and beautiful dunes, Woolacombe is popular with visitors who flock to this attractive seaside town each year. It has both European Union Blue Flag and Premier Seaside Beach awards in recognition of its consistent cleanliness, water quality and good facilities. It is also a popular destination with surfers. In 1944 Woolacombe doubled up for the Normandy beaches in the run up to D-Day, becoming a practice ground for US forces honing their amphibious landing techniques.

Ilfracombe *left*

The small harbour at Ilfracombe stands out from this high vantage point on the nearby cliffs. The town is home to an Iron Age fort established by the *Dumnonii* – the dominant Celtic tribe in this part of south-west Britain. The harbour culminates in high ground – Lantern Hill is topped by a small chapel dedicated to St Nicholas, thought to be the oldest working lighthouse in the UK. Ilfracombe was an important port in the 13th century, supplying shipping needed in a number of the military adventures of King John, including the Siege of Calais.

Uphill near Weston-Super-Mare *above*

The small village of Uphill is situated just outside the busy seaside resort of Weston-Super-Mare. It was settled long before the Roman invasion and it thrived under the Romans too, probably as a fort. Its most venerable building is the Old Church of St Nicholas which was built around 1066, probably on the site of an earlier Saxon church. For centuries it has been a landmark to sailors navigating the dangerous currents of the bay.

Weston-Super-Mare *left*

Eighteen miles south-west of Bristol, Weston is known for its sandy beaches and traditional seaside attractions and entertainments. At low tide the distance between land and sea can be as much as a mile which accounts for the considerable length of the town's Grand Pier which dates from 1904. Weston has a number of famous "sons and daughters" including Roald Dahl, Jill Dando and John Cleese.

Porlock *above*

A spectacular view from Exmoor across Porlock to the coast and the Bristol Channel. The little village of Porlock nestles in a hollow below Exmoor; access to the village is via Porlock Hill, a road with a series of hairpin bends and a 1-in-4 gradient. Near the sea is Porlock Ridge and Saltmarsh nature reserve, a Site of Special Scientific Interest created when the lowland behind a high shingle embankment was breached by the sea in the 1990s. Two miles west of the village within beautiful woodland is the church of St Culborne – just 35ft long, it is the smallest church in England. Porlock has strong associations with the Romantic poets – William Wordsworth and Samuel Taylor Coleridge roamed the North Somerset countryside, and after one of his epic walks Coleridge had a vision in which a "person from Porlock" appeared before him; when transcribed, it became 54 lines of *Kubla Khan*, one of his most famous poems.

East Quantoxhead *left*

The beach at East Quantoxhead, near Porlock, is an excellent place to look for fossils. Among the remains of extinct creatures found in the rocks on the shoreline are ammonites, nautilus' shells and many other marine creatures that lived in the seas over 200 million years ago.

East Anglia and Lincolnshire

Wide open skies, reed-fringed marshes and magnificent beaches characterise the coastline of East Anglia and Lincolnshire, from Essex to the Humber. The Essex coastline is dotted with creeks and river valleys graced with beautiful towns and villages such as Maldon and Tollesbury. The Suffolk coast has some of the best seaside towns in Britain – with Aldeburgh, Southwold and Walberswick among them. The vast network of overlapping waterways and lakes of the Broads provide Norfolk with a unique landscape while to the north, the "quiet beauty" of the Lincolnshire coast has provided inspiration for artists and writers, including the poet John Betjeman.

Southend-on-Sea *right*
Deckchairs for hire on the front at Southend-on-Sea are caught in the glorious late afternoon light. Just 42 miles from London, situated on the Thames where the river broadens out into the sea, Southend is a perennial favourite. The Victorians "discovered" Southend once the railways opened up the possibility of day-trips to ordinary Londoners. Among the attractions that developed to cater for the needs of the holidaymakers was Southend Pier – at a length of one and a third miles, it is the longest pleasure pier in the world. Visitors can take a diesel-hydraulic railway trip to the end or walk its length – out of season, on a foggy day, this can be quite an eerie experience, suspended between the land and the sea.

West Mersea *left*
Gaily painted beach huts grace the beach at West Mersea. Located in the estuary of the rivers Blackwater and the Colne, Mersea is the most easterly settled island in England. It is connected to the mainland by a causeway called the Strood. Its sandy beaches only become muddy some distance from the shore, in contrast to some of the beaches on the inlets and estuaries of the Essex coast.

Wivenhoe *above*

The picturesque town of Wivenhoe seen from across the river Colne. Located one mile from Colchester, its pubs and town centre are popular with students from nearby Essex university, whose main campus is at Wivenhoe Park. The prominent tower in the photograph is that of St Mary the Virgin – a church with pre-Norman roots which was substantially rebuilt and enlarged in 1850 following a fire. Wivenhoe has an important maritime history with a tradition of shipbuilding and repair that dates back centuries. During the Second World War its shipyard was frantically busy, converting drifters and trawlers to minesweepers and repairing other marine craft. By the 60s the yard had closed and the future of the site was uncertain. Recently many of the old buildings have been absorbed into the Wivenhoe Conservation Area.

Brightlingsea *left*

The ancient port of Brightlingsea lies at the mouth of the river Colne. One of its earliest roles was the defence of Colchester, further up the river, and it is the only Cinque Port north of the Thames. Today it is a typical south-east seaside resort with colourful beach huts, a children's paddling pool and a sandy beach. Its main industry was fishing and the town's local oysters were sought after. It is very popular with recreational sailors and the Brightlingsea Sailing Club has an active membership.

Maldon *above*

Located east of Colchester on the Blackwater
estuary, the historic town of Maldon was, for
centuries, one of just two towns in the county of
Essex. King Edward the Elder lived here in the
eighth century while Danish settlers were intent
on over-running the whole of East Anglia; the Old
English epic poem *The Battle of Maldon* chronicles
the Anglo-Saxon defeat in AD991 by a force of
invading Vikings. The battle is commemorated by
a bronze statue, erected in 2006, of Byrhtnoth, the
Saxon warrior who perished in the battle. Today
Maldon is a peaceful market town with a
picturesque quay; it is the home of the famous
brown-sailed Thames sailing barges and a lively
yachting community, for whom the tower and
spike of St Mary's church is a landmark as they sail
back up river.

Tollesbury *right*

A row of weatherboarded sail lofts at Tollesbury,
situated on the mouth of the Blackwater estuary,
east of Maldon. The village signpost shows a
plough and a sail; the sail lofts are a potent
reminder that the village has derived as much
benefit from the sea as agriculture over the
centuries. The village featured in the 2006 BBC
series *Restoration Village* for its efforts to restore the
listed Woodrolfe Granary, a weatherboarded
building overlooking the estuary and saltmarshes.

Walton-on-the-Naze *right*

To the north of the small but busy resort town of
Walton-on-the-Naze is the "naze" itself – a peninsula
well-known for its wildlife and Hanoverian tower. This
beautiful area faces destruction because of ceaseless
erosion and it is thought that within 50 years the tower
will have crumbled and fallen to the beach below,
despite the coastal defences that have been erected
here. The nearby Hamford Marshes feature as the
location of Arthur Ransome's *Secret Water*, the eighth
title in the *Swallows and Amazons* series.

Harwich *right*

The historic port of Harwich developed as a result
of its location between the Thames and the Humber.
Situated at the confluence of the rivers Stour and
Orwell, it became an important naval base in 1657,
during the Commonwealth of Oliver Cromwell.
Among the town's famous historic figures are Samuel
Pepys, who was the local MP, and Christopher Jones,
the master of the *Mayflower*. The town contains both
important medieval and 18th-century buildings
including the Grade I listed Guild Hall of 1769.
The Electric Palace Cinema (1911) in Harwich is one
of the oldest purpose-built cinemas to have survived
in the UK complete with its original projection room.
Today Harwich is a major container port and
a departure point for ferries heading to the Hook
of Holland and Denmark.

Aldeburgh *right*

Located on the Suffolk coast north-east of the county town of Ipswich, Aldeburgh was once a hub of the Elizabethan and Jacobean naval world. It was then a major shipbuilding centre, its yards producing *The Golden Hind* with which Drake circled the world and also *The Sea Venture* – flagship of the Virginia Company. The silting up of the river Alde put paid to all that and for many years the town had to rely on its fishing industry. Then in the 19th century Aldeburgh gained a new lease of life as a holiday resort. The poet George Crabbe was born in Aldeburgh in 1754 and the town is thought to have inspired his poems *The Village* and *The Borough*. In 1948 the composer Benjamin Britten and the singer Peter Pears founded the Aldeburgh music festival, with concerts held at the nearby Maltings in Snape.

Shingle Street *below*

South of Aldeburgh, on the Suffolk Heritage Coast, the tiny hamlet of Shingle Street is a bleak spot with a mysterious history. Nearby Orford Ness was used for all sorts of clandestine military activities from the 1930s up until the 1960s. During the Second World War Shingle Street was evacuated and the area heavily mined. It was at Orford Ness that radar was first tested. Local stories about the thwarting of a German invasion in 1940 by setting the sea on fire off Orford Ness and the beaches being littered with bodies have long persisted, though it seems now the story was quite possibly propaganda spread at a time when Britain was extremely vulnerable to invasion.

Southwold *right*

At the mouth of the river Blyth, the little town of Southwold has had a troubled history. It lost its status as a major fishing port thanks to the gradual appearance of a shingle bar across the harbour mouth. In 1659 the town was largely burnt down and some of Southwold's open "greens" date back to that conflagration. Its beachfront is graced with colourful huts, a decommissioned lighthouse and a lively Victorian pier that was substantially refurbished in 2001. George Orwell's parents lived in the town and he was a frequent visitor up until 1939. Today Southwold is a fashionable resort.

Dunwich *below*

In the early middle ages Dunwich, north of Aldeburgh, was one of the largest ports in western Europe with a population of more than 3,000 and eight churches. In 1286 a large storm swept much of the town into the sea and the river was partly silted up. The harbour went next in another storm in 1328 and over 400 houses were lost in a tempest in 1347. The same process of erosion and loss has continued ever since and today all eight churches have vanished. Legend has it that in storms it is possible to still hear church bells ringing beneath the waves. The land near Dunwich is now a nature reserve.

Orford *above*

Built by Henry II in an attempt to keep the then Earl of Norfolk, Hugh Bigod, under control and to protect the coast, the Great Tower of Orford Castle stands guard over Orford Ness. The structure is unique among British castles as it consists of a circular central portion flanked by three turrets. Orford Ness is a shingle spit formed by longshore drift on the Suffolk coast, divided from the mainland by the river Alde. It is thought that much of the material that makes up the spit has been plucked from further up the coast, as far away as Dunwich.

Snape Maltings *left*

The Maltings at Snape consists of a magnificent collection of 19th-century granaries and malthouses on the banks of the river Alde. Originally used for the brewing of beer, the maltings closed in 1960. They have since been converted into a world-class concert hall in which the main events of the annual Aldeburgh Festival are staged. Nearby is the Holst Library named after Imogen, the daughter of composer Gustav Holst. She was a friend of Benjamin Britten, the founder with Peter Pears of the Aldeburgh Festival and its artistic director from 1956 to 1977.

Sizewell *below*

This small fishing village near Thorpeness is the location of two nuclear power stations – Sizewell A and Sizewell B. Sizewell A started to generate power in 1966 and houses two 1000 megawatt Magnox reactors. It is reaching the end of its life and is due to be decommissioned at a cost of over £1bn. Sizewell B is the UK's only large pressurised water reactor and was built between 1988 and 1995. The dome of Sizewell B still packs a dramatic punch when observed from a distance down the coast.

Thorpeness *left*

Evening peace falls on the Mere at Thorpeness – a coastal village south of Dunwich. It was once just a small fishing hamlet but in 1910 its character changed when it and much of the surrounding land was bought by Stuart Ogilvie, an immensely rich barrister. He turned the place into his own pet project creating what has been called a "private fantasy holiday village". Among the structures Ogilvie commissioned were a country club and a disguised water tower called "the House in the Clouds". Thorpeness is a quiet village of about 400 people in the winter, but its population climbs to more than 1,500 in summer. One highlight is the annual August regatta which is followed by a fireworks display.

Lowestoft *right & below*

The Suffolk coastal town of Lowestoft is sandwiched between the Norfolk Broads and the North Sea. The town's fortunes are founded on the sea; its gently sloping sandy beaches meant that it was able to develop as a seaside resort from the mid 19th century onwards, while fishing – particularly herring fishing – had been the lifeblood of the town for centuries. In the middle ages, rivalry with nearby Great Yarmouth over the herring fisheries was fierce and the towns subsequently took opposite sides in the English Civil War with Lowestoft supporting the Royalist cause. The town owes its modern-day success to the entrepreneur Sir Samuel Morton Peto who helped establish rail links with Norwich and beyond. It suffered in the Second World War when it became a key navigation point on the coast for German bombers, and a frequent target. In fact more bombs per head of population were dropped here than anywhere else in Britain.

Great Yarmouth *above*

Children enjoy a traditional Punch and Judy show on the sands at Great Yarmouth, Norfolk. The town has some beautiful historic buildings which include a 17th-century merchant's house. Behind South Quay there is a maze of alleys and lanes known as "The Rows", which also feature in an exhibit in the award-winning Time and Tide Museum, which occupies one of the town's most substantial herring smokehouses.

Norfolk Broads *right and below*

Horsey Windmill (right) and Runham Swim Windmill (below) are two much photographed sights on The Broads – a network of overlapping rivers and lakes that straddle the border of Norfolk and Suffolk. With a total area of 117 square miles and over 125 miles of navigable waterways, they are Britain's largest area of wetland. It is only recently that the Broads' origins have been established. Once thought to be a natural feature they are now known to be the flooded remains of early peat excavations. Under the Norfolk and Suffolk Broads Act of 1988 they have been given special protection, and their status is similar to that of a national park. The Broads are a favourite boating holiday destination and are Britain's largest protected wetland, home to numerous bird species including several kinds of goose. Britain's only breeding Common Cranes are found in the area.

Waxham *right*

Visitors to the coastal hamlet of Waxham have only to cross the dunes to reach its long sandy beach and, if fortunate, catch sight of a seal swimming in the shallows. Waxham's major attraction is the 16th-century tithe barn (one of the largest in the country) which was built by the Woodhouse family using the remains of the two monasteries they had bought following Henry VIII's dissolution of the monasteries. It is now owned by Norfolk County Council and has been refurbished with special protection laid down for the colony of rare bats that have settled there.

Mundesley *below*

A wooden groyne projects across the beach and into the sea near Mundesley – a small village on Norfolk's north-east coast. It was once an important port and a popular Victorian resort but coastal erosion has destroyed the railway connection and the beach is littered with sections of fallen track. Mundesley's war memorial celebrates the sailors and volunteers who cleared the North Sea of mines during and after the Second World War.

Cromer

Well into the 19th century Cromer, on the north coast of Norfolk, was little more than a fishing village; it became fashionable in the early 19th century when a clutch of rich Norwich banking families made it their summer home. The development of the railway hastened Cromer's expansion, bringing visitors keen to enjoy its beautiful beaches. Today Cromer is famous for its pier and its seafood – the Cromer crab is a famous local delicacy. The parish church of St Peter and St Paul dominates the skyline – it has a magnificent Burne-Jones stained-glass window, plus modern stained-glass commemorating the town's seafarers; its 160ft (49m) tower is the highest in the county. Cromer is renowned for its two lifeboats which, over the years, have carried out a number of significant rescues.

Brancaster Staithe *left*

Bags of fresh mussels await collection on the mudflats near Brancaster Staithe. The land around the village is a mix of sand, mudflats and saltmarsh and is protected by the National Trust. A petrified forest can be seen on the shore near Brancaster at low tide. The Romans built a fort here called *Branodunum*, garrisoned by troops from Dalmatia (today's Croatia and Montenegro).

Hunstanton *below left*

"Sunny Hunny" as it is known locally is a popular seaside town in Norfolk on the easternmost lip of the Wash. Because it faces west it is the only English east coast resort to enjoy sunsets over the sea. Hunstanton is famous for its colourful striped cliffs, a combination of reddish standstone topped by chalk. This unique cliff formation is popular with fossil-hunters.

Thornham Creek *right*

An idyllic spot on the saltmarshes of north-west Norfolk, Thornham Creek has miles of open beaches fringed with sand dunes, plus chalk and sandstone cliffs. The nearby village of Thornham is the perfect base for walkers and nature-lovers, and the adjoining reserve at Holme is internationally important for its birds and mammals – ringed plover, oystercatchers and little tern nest on its shingle ridges, while redshank, avocet and snipe breed on the grazing marshes. In the autumn large numbers of wildfowl arrive – to spend the winter feeding on the saltmarshes; they can be viewed from hides.

Morston Marshes *left*

This atmospheric part of the north Norfolk coast is protected by the National Trust; it consists of a maze of creeks and mudflats supporting maritime plants such as sea lavender and attracts many birds. Spring migrants include chiffchaffs, wheatears and sandwich terns. By the end of April the reedbed is full of reed and sedge warblers while the extended autumn migration sees the pools occupied by green and wood sandpiper, greenshank, whimbrel and little ringed plover.

King's Lynn *right*

Located on the Great Ouse near where it enters the Wash, King's Lynn is the third largest town in Norfolk. Its prosperity is founded on the sea and as a port in the middle ages it rivalled Bruges and Bristol. The town began to decline in the 18th century but its fortunes improved again with the arrival of the railways in 1847. In 1985 the historic heart of King's Lynn was used for scenes of 18th-century New York in the film *Revolution*.

Terrington Marsh *above*

Terrington Marsh is a tranquil spot to the south of the Wash. Its main local settlement is Terrington St Clement – extending over 13 square miles, it is said to be the largest village in Norfolk. In the Second World War an entirely bogus airfield was created on Terrington Marsh using an elaborate array of lights as a decoy target for German bombers seeking the nearby real airfield at Sutton Bridge. It was a highly successful ploy and Terrington Marsh was bombed heavily on a number of occasions, with no cost to military infrastructure – the only damage being to local potato fields.

Huttoft *left*

The quiet beauty of the Lincolnshire coast is seen here at Huttoft, nine miles north of Skegness. Huttoft is recommended by surfers as being a good winter beach when the wind is from the west. John Betjeman loved the county, and Huttoft provided the inspiration for his poem *A Lincolnshire Church*. The main feature of the village is a sailless windmill – a major local landmark in the flat landscape.

Humber Estuary *above*

To the Anglo-Saxons the substantial tidal estuary of the Humber marked the dividing line between the northern and southern kingdoms. Today it forms the boundary between the East Riding of Yorkshire to the north and Lincolnshire to the south. The Humber is dotted with major ports including Hull, Grimsby and Immingham; today, these are connected by the magnificent Humber Bridge, which opened in 1981.

Skegness *left*

Low winter sun casts a warm light over the beach at Skegness in winter. To the south is the nature reserve at Gibraltar Point, an area of unspoilt coastline with important plant and animal communities. The coastline here is of great scientific interest and is made up of sandy and muddy seashore, sand dune, saltmarsh and freshwater habitats. The reserve extends for a distance of about three miles along the coast from the southern end of Skegness to the entrance to the Wash.

Cleethorpes *right*

Every May kite enthusiasts from all over the world descend on Cleethorpes, at the mouth of the Humber, to take part in a two-day festival which includes night-flying and a firework finale.

Yorkshire

The Yorkshire coast's remarkable "craggy grandeur" makes it both inspiring and dangerous. Historically its villages and towns thrived on the sea industries of fishing, whaling and smuggling. With the arrival of the railways in Victorian times seaside visitors flocked to the coast, followed by artists and writers. Today, the coastline that forms the eastern edge of the North York Moors national park has been re-branded as the North Yorkshire Heritage Coast. The Cleveland Way long-distance footpath hugs the clifftops from Saltburn in the north to Filey in the south.

Bridlington *above*

The miniature "land train" makes its way along the front at Bridlington's North Bay. This classic seaside resort benefits from nearby natural wonders, which include Bempton Cliffs and Flamborough Head, clearly visible from the north beach. Another local attraction is Sewerby Hall with its beautiful park and gardens.

Bempton Cliffs *right*

Crevasses in the spectacular Bempton Cliffs provide the perfect environment for large colonies of seabirds. The area is owned and protected by the RSPB. About 10 per cent of the UK's kittiwake population live and breed on Bempton Cliffs. The large puffin population is said to be threatened due to the impact global warming may have on the sand eels upon which they depend but there is still a large summer colony here and they can be spotted setting off and returning from fishing trips on the Dogger Bank some 25 miles out to sea.

Flamborough Head *above* **Thornwick Nab** *below*

Jutting out into the North Sea and home to large populations of seabirds, the seven-mile long headland at Flamborough Head between Filey and Bridlington is one of the North Yorkshire coastline's best-known natural wonders. A benign spot on a warm summer day, this can be a ferocious part of the coast and has been the site of numerous shipwrecks. In 1674 action was taken and the result was Britain's oldest lighthouse. It is the only known example of a beacon lighthouse in England, where a huge brazier on top would be used as a light. There is no evidence it was ever used, and a new lighthouse was built on the cliffs in 1806. It was just off the coast in 1779 that the US sea commander John Paul Jones made his name in an engagement with British ships during the American War of Independence, managing to capture the Royal Naval vessel *The Countess of Scarborough*. At low tide beneath the cliffs at Nab Close (right) a spectacular wave-cut platform is exposed.

Filey *right and below*

Fishing boats line the Coble Landing in Filey, the elegant resort to the south of Scarborough. The town benefits from five miles of sandy beaches which are protected to the north by Filey Brigg, a finger of gritstone which projects one-mile into the sea forming a natural pier and breakwater. In a superb position looking out over the bay, Filey was transformed from a small fishing village into a "planned" town in the early 19th century. The view below is of Filey North Cliff and Grisethorpe Cliffs beyond.

Scarborough

Its stunning location and sandy beaches meant that Scarborough was well-placed to become Britain's first seaside resort. The Grand Hotel (right) was completed in 1867 and was, at the time, one of the largest hotels in the world. Its four towers represented the seasons and its 12 floors the months of the year. The town dates back to the mid-10th century. It suffered from Viking raids and was burnt down prior to the Norman invasion, only recovering in the reign of Edward II. In the middle ages the famous Scarborough Fair lasted for six weeks and people flocked to it from all over Europe. The headland (below) with the ruined Norman castle separates North Bay from the South.

The chairlift

Scarborough's South Bay is the main focus of the resort and contains many arcades and entertainment facilities. The North Bay has traditionally been "the quiet end" of the town although it also has its attractions such as the chairlift (above) and Peasholm Park, which features a mock maritime battle re-enacted on the boating lake with large model boats and fireworks throughout the summer holiday season.

69

Robin Hood's Bay

The picturesque fishing village of Robin Hood's Bay is in an isolated spot, bounded on three sides by marshy moorland – one of the reasons perhaps why the local people were able to make a healthy living throughout the 17th and 18th centuries from smuggling. Tunnels below the houses which line the steep winding streets were used in the 18th century for smuggling goods ashore; everywhere there is the sound of gulls which nest on the rooftops and chimneystacks. In the 19th century the twin attractions of the area's rugged beauty and fossil-hunting drew the first visitors – Boggle Hole (right), half a mile south of the town, is a wonderful place to search for fossils and explore rock pools.

Whitby *left and below left*

Named as Best Seaside Resort 2006 by *Holiday Which* magazine, Whitby has a long history. The first major structure there was religious – an abbey was built and Whitby later became a centre of learning thanks to its first abbess Hilda. By early modern times the town's fortunes were more commercial – the export of coal and alum. It was also a shipbuilding centre and, by the late 18th century, a thriving whaling port. It was in Whitby that Captain James Cook, the naval explorer, learned the maritime trade and there is a museum dedicated to him in the town. The view (left) is across the harbour to East Cliff and St Hilda's Abbey.

Staithes *above*

Known locally as "Steers", Staithes is a seaside village at the most northerly point of the North Yorkshire coast. The stream or "beck" that runs through the town is the border between North Yorkshire and Redcar and Cleveland. Once a thriving fishing port, Staithes now relies mainly on tourism. The ancient cliffs around Staithes are a source of rare fossils. The village has a reputation as an artists' colony and was even home to its own "group", known as the Northern Impressionists, which included Dame Laura Knight. Staithes' most famous son was Captain Cook who worked here as a grocer's apprentice between 1745-1746.

North-East England

The coastline of north-east England stretches from the Scottish border to the banks of the river Tees. In between it encompasses the estuaries of the rivers Tees, Wear and Tyne including the industrial heartlands of Middlesbrough, Sunderland and Newcastle. To the north lies the beautiful unspoilt countryside of Northumberland, which includes the stunning castles of Dunstanburgh and Bamburgh, and the exquisite Lindisfarne, with its castle and ruined priory.

Roker Pier *right*
The view south-east from Sunderland shows the red and white Roker lighthouse and pier almost entirely obscured during a violent storm. The lighthouse was built in 1903 at the instructions of the Earl of Durham. It is 75ft (23m) high and its light flashes out to sea every five seconds. The pier is popular with local anglers, who will brave the most dangerous conditions to cast their lines. On occasion coastguards have had to use the emergency tunnel which runs under the 2,800ft long pier to bring people to safety.

Saltburn-by-the-Sea

Old Saltburn was a modest fishing village which, for over 150 years, was reputedly one of the north-east coast's main smuggling communities. It was a remote place and its hidden beaches, steep cliffs and woods all provided good cover for nefarious activities. In 1859 Henry Pease, son of the founder of the Stockton and Darlington Railway, was staying with his brother at Marske. On an evening walk to Old Saltburn he experienced a "vision" and explained that, when seated on the hillside he had seen, on the edge of the cliff before him, "a town arise and the quiet unfrequented glen turned into a lovely garden". Pease founded the town, giving the streets fairy-tale names – Ruby, Emerald, Garnet, Pearl and Diamond. Attractions include the pier (left). Hunt Cliffs (right) show the characteristic red of strata rich in iron – there are many disused iron mines in the area.

73

South Shields *left*

A ferry plies its way across placid water on its way to dock in South Shields at the mouth of the river Tyne. South Shields has six miles of coastline and three miles of river frontage, dominated by the massive piers at the mouth of the Tyne. As well as being the largest town in South Tyneside, South Shields is also the region's most popular seaside resort, and is marketed as a part of Catherine Cookson Country.

Whitburn Coastal Park *below*

The wind and sea-etched cliffs along the South Tyneside coast (now the Whitburn Coastal Park) are testament to serious coastal erosion. Once the village of Marsden stood near here but when Whitburn Colliery closed in 1968 many families moved to modern houses nearby and the decision was taken to demolish the village as it lay in the path of the retreating cliffs.

Souter Lighthouse *left*

The southern end of Marsden Bay is overlooked by the red-and white-striped Souter Lightouse, the first lighthouse in Britain to power its light and foghorn using an alternating electric current. Now owned by the National Trust it receives many visitors who are able to see its engine room and experience at first-hand the cramped and Spartan living quarters provided for the original keepers.

St Mary's Lighthouse, Whitley Bay *below*

Just eight miles from Newcastle, Whitley Bay's main attractions are its glorious golden sands and St Mary's Island, which can only be reached across a causeway at low tide. The lighthouse started work in 1897 and remained in operation until 1984 when it was superseded by modern navigational techniques. North Tyneside Council now operates the lighthouse as a visitor centre.

Alnmouth *right*

This view north-west along the Northumberland coast shows the picturesque village of Alnmouth with the blue of Alnmouth Bay beyond. It was a shipbuilding centre in the 13th century but was almost wiped out by successive disasters – the raiding Scots in 1336 and the Black Death in 1348. The town's recovery took several centuries and by the 17th century it was a prosperous port again. A storm on Christmas Eve 1806 changed the town's fortunes by diverting the course of the river Aln. This blow was eased somewhat by the town's rising popularity as a resort – a trend that continues today.

Beadnell Bay *below*

The substantial pele tower at the centre of Beadnell is a reminder of times when the border lands between Scotland and England were hotly contested. Beadnell Bay is a far more tranquil spot today. At the northern end of the sandy beach is the harbour with its distinctive limekilns, used for lime production in the 1820s.

Dunstanburgh *above*

There can be few more spectacular sights on the English coastline than the ruins of 14th-century Dunstanburgh Castle. It was once one of the most formidable strongholds in the north and its grandeur is still apparent despite its ruinous state. One of the best ways to reach the castle today is across the rocky beach; on rougher days the wind and sea provide a suitable accompaniment to this magnificent scene.

Farne Islands *right*

Depending on the tides and sea levels there are between 18 and 25 islands in the Farne group. Located off the Northumberland coast, this is one of Britain's foremost bird sanctuaries. The islands have a key place in the history of Christianity, as they were the retreat of St Cuthbert, the bishop of Lindisfarne. In old age he returned to his beloved island of Inner Farne, dying there in 687. Longstone is the furthest-flung of the Farnes and is associated with Grace Darling, whose heroism during the rescue of survivors of the steamer *Forfashire* – which ran aground in September 1838 – made her world-famous.

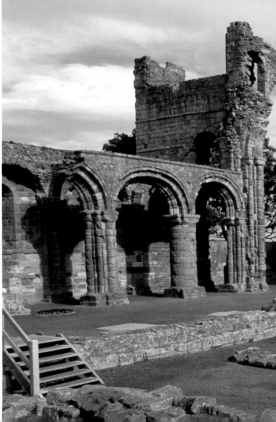

Bamburgh Castle *above*

The impregnable stronghold of Bamburgh Castle is perched on a huge rock, visible for miles around on the Northumbrian coast. It dominates the pretty village below, which clusters around the castle. The local churchyard has a monument to Grace Darling, together with the graves of victims of shipwrecks on the nearby Farne Islands. Bamburgh was the tribal stronghold of an ancient British tribe called the *Votadini* who stood out against the Vikings. The name originates from the time of Aethelfrith, the first King of Northumbria, who named the fortress or "burgh" after his wife, Bebba. Bamburgh Castle was heavily restored during Victoria's reign by the Newcastle-born industrialist William, Lord Armstrong. In 1971 Bamburgh was chosen as Macbeth's stronghold in the film version of the play directed by Roman Polanski.

Berwick-upon-Tweed *below*

Between 1147 and 1482 Berwick changed hands between Scotland and England over 13 times: today it is firmly located in the English county of Northumberland. Situated on the mouth of the river Tweed, Berwick is the most northerly town in England. The town's architecure is suitably military and defensive given its tempestuous past; much of it is enclosed by walls constructed in 1596 at the time of Elizabeth I. The architectural historian Nikolaus Pevsner loved Berwick, describing it as "one of the most exciting towns in the country, with scarcely an irritating building anywhere".

Lindisfarne *left and above left*

To the north of Bamburgh lies Holy Island or Lindisfarne (to use its more ancient name) seen here with its dramatic castle. Lindisfarne is separated from the mainland at high tides and can only be reached by its causeway. The Norman priory stands on the site of an Anglo-Saxon monastery founded by St Aidan in 635. Aidan is believed to have chosen the island because of its isolation and proximity to the Northumbrian capital at Bamburgh; it proved a strategic spot from which he could launch his campaign to convert Northumberland to Christianity. In the mid 7th century Cuthbert became the fifth bishop of Lindisfarne and further built the island's reputation thanks to his ability to heal the sick and work miracles. The castle was converted into a private residence by the architect Sir Edwin Lutyens in 1903. It has been a National Trust property since 1944.

Wales

Few regions of Britain can boast such a beautiful and varied coastline within a relatively compact area. In the north, the popular seaside resorts of Llandudno, Prestatyn and Colwyn Bay rub shoulders with fortified towns such as Caernarfon and Conwy. In the west there are remote beaches with historic centres such as Harlech and St Davids. In the south, the Gower peninsula between Llanelli and Swansea was the first place in Britain to be designated as an Area of Outstanding Natural Beauty. And the great cities of Cardiff and Swansea, once marked by their industrial heritage, now boast highly acclaimed quayside developments with new landmark buildings and restored gems from the country's industrial past.

Cardiff Bay *above*

Cardiff Bay has been transformed in recent years. Once an industrial landscape consisting of docks which specialised in handling coal and iron, it declined in the years after the Second World War, becoming a place of abandoned warehouses and mudflats. Crucial to the regeneration of the area has been the construction of a barrage that now maintains regular water levels instead of the wide tidal fluctuations that used to render the harbour unusable for large parts of each day. The Bay has seen other huge construction projects including the Wales Millennium Centre, an exciting new venue for music, opera, concerts and other events; opened in 2004, its curved roof looms behind the historic redbrick Pierhead Building.

Nash Point, Glamorgan *left*

Nash Point lies on the Glamorgan Heritage Coast. The rocks along this shore are considered unique – a combination of Liassic limestone and carboniferous sandstone. The strata were laid down over 200 million years ago when most of Wales lay beneath the surface of a warm Jurassic sea. These grey-yellow cliffs face out to sea, bearing the brunt of Atlantic onshore winds. Many ships have come to grief here. One of the most recent disasters occurred in 1962 when an oil tanker crashed into Nash Point – its crew only escaping thanks to the efforts of the Bristol Channel lifeboat team.

Three Cliffs Bay *right*

This beautiful bay on the Gower Peninsula is widely regarded as one of Britain's best. Located just to the west of Swansea, it takes its name from the three attractive limestone cliffs that jut out into the sea. The three stunning tracts of golden sand are all connected, but visitors can only walk from one to the other at low tide. The wind-battered ruins of Pennard Castle stand guard over the area on a nearby hill.

Swansea Bay *left & above*

Swansea Bay (seen on the left from a vantage point on Kilvey Hill) is an inlet of the Bristol Channel. It was once an important area for fishing and its oysters were legendary, but in the early 20th century pollution and over-fishing destroyed the beds. The height of Swansea's fame came during the Industrial Revolution; in the 19th century it was the biggest exporter of coal in the world. But the city suffered in the Second World War and lost much of its historic centre. Today it is a vibrant and exciting city, proud of its cultural heritage – the new maritime quarter (above) houses the National Waterfront Museum celebrating Wales' history of industry and innovation; every autumn the city hosts a festival in honour of Dylan Thomas, Swansea's most famous son.

Mumbles Head *left*

The curious name of the headland at the tip of Swansea Bay may derive from the old French word *mamelles*, meaning "breasts", which the two islets at the end of the Mumbles headland resemble. Mumbles Lighthouse stands on the furthest islet. The first such structure here went up in 1794. Originally, its light was provided by braziers. Later there was a switch to an oil lantern and since 1934 the present lighthouse has been fully automated. In 1995 it had its most recent refit – gaining solar panels and emergency monitoring equipment. The pretty village of Mumbles is a popular seaside resort – there are wonderful views across the Bristol Channel and its steep streets are full of restaurants, pubs and coffee shops.

Langland Bay *below*

The beautiful sandy bay of Langland is a brisk 15-minute walk from Mumbles and is a popular spot with locals and visitors. Langland is a place of pilgrimage for keen surfers owing to offshore reefs such as Crab Island, the Sand Bar, Middle Reef and the Lefts. To the east are situated the equally attractive Caswell Bay, with its sandy beach, and Limeslade. The Glamorgan coastal path starts at Mumbles and links all the major beaches of the Gower Peninsula.

Worms Head, Rhossili *above*

With its three-mile long sandy beach, views out over Worms Head and frequent spectacular sunsets over the Atlantic, Rhossili Bay is one of the most dramatic stretches of Britain's coastline. The cliffs and beach are managed by the National Trust and so development here is restricted – the village consists of a church, a pub, and some tea rooms. The beach is reached by a stepped path behind the pub, while the best way to appreciate the whole sweep of the bay is to walk west over the soft, grazed grass to the tip of the headland. Worms Head is connected to the mainland by a causeway which is passable for two hours either side of low tide.

St Non's Bay *right*

The stunning bay of St Non's is part of the rugged St Davids Peninsula, just 10 minutes walk from the city of St Davids. It is on the Pembrokeshire Coastal Path and is a place of pilgrimage – legend has it that it was at this spot in 500 that Non gave birth to David, the patron saint of Wales. She is said to have been violated by a certain Sanctus, a king of Ceredigion, and in due course gave birth to the baby boy. The ruined chapel of St Non is cared for by Welsh Heritage and there is a retreat house nearby. During the thunderstorm that heralded St David's birth it is reported that a spring first emerged nearby and this too became a venerated spot with people dropping offerings into the holy well constructed on the spot. The spring's waters were believed to have had miraculous powers for healing eye diseases.

Tenby *below*

In Welsh Tenby is *Dinbych-y-Pysgod* or the "little town of the fishes". The town grew around the now ruined remains of the town's castle which stands on a high rocky headland overlooking the resort's two beaches. Today Tenby offers the visitor a host of interesting sights including its 13th-century town walls and a Tudor merchant's house. The fort on St Catherine's Island was built in the 1860s to protect the coast from the threat of a French invasion. Just off the coast lies Caldey Island, once a Benedictine settlement, now a reformed Cistercian monastery.

Dylan Thomas' Boathouse, Laugharne *below*

For the last four years of his life, Wales' most famous modern poet Dylan Thomas (1914-53) lived with his wife Caitlin and their three children in the Boathouse on the edge of the "heron priested" Taf Estuary. The home was gifted to the poet by Margaret Taylor who wanted Thomas to live in Wales.

It is here that he composed many of his most famous works including *Under Milk Wood* in which the fictitious Llareggub drew direct inspiration from nearby Laugharne. The Boathouse is now a heritage centre – the second main point of call by Dylan fans following a visit to his grave alongside that of Caitlin in the local churchyard.

St Davids *left*

St Davids is the smallest city in Britain. It has a population of just over 2,000 but the presence of a cathedral means it has "city" status. The cathedral stands on the site of Glyn Rhosyn – the monastery that St David founded in 530. St Davids is considered the spiritual heart of Wales and, isolated though it might be today on the Pembrokshire coast, the city once enjoyed great importance as a major meeting point for ships carrying pilgrims back and forth from Ireland, Cornwall and Brittany. Today St Davids is the only city in Britain that is located within a national park – the Pembrokeshire Coast National Park.

Whitesands Bay *above*

A view north over Whitesands Bay with the mountainous St Davids Head in the distance. The area is rich in ancient burial monuments and field systems. The Blue Flag award-winning bay itself is today enjoyed by walkers and surfers. The city of St Davids is just two miles away.

St Justinian's *right*

Legend has it that the body of St Justinian – the Byzantine emperor and saint – was brought to Wales and landed here on the Pembrokeshire coast. There is a nearby chapel dedicated to him although there is no public access. Today, as well as being a spot for walkers and climbers, St Justinian's is (in the summer) important as the point of departure for ferries carrying visitors to see the bird and grey seal colonies at Ramsay Island. The island is also one of the best sites in Wales to see choughs and other breeding species including ravens, buzzards, peregrines, wheatears, gulls and auks. In addition to the ferry harbour, St Justinian's is home to the local lifeboat station – the red building in the photograph.

Fishguard *left*

The harbour at Fishguard is dotted with pleasure craft in this view from the south-east, taken from the heights above Goodwick Quay. The mouth of the river Gwaun around which the town has grown up can just be seen to the right of the photograph. The town, as its name implies, was once an important fishing centre and had a very active herring fleet. Its harbour is now the place to catch ferries to Rosslare in Ireland. In 1797 an ill-conceived and poorly-executed French invasion of Britain finally petered out in Fishguard with the surrender being signed by the French commander, an American called Colonel William Tate, in the Royal Oak pub. This attractive pub, located in the market square, is today a lively venue for music.

Strumble Head

The lighthouse at Strumble Head sits atop Ynysmeicl (St Michael's Island) an islet to the west of Fisghguard. It was built in 1908 to help protect shipping travelling between the new harbour at Fishguard and Ireland; this stretch of coast was particularly treacherous, and 60 ships perished here in the 19th century. In 2003 the wreck of an 18th century French vessel was discovered in the nearby seas and it is thought that it may have been one of the invasion fleet of 1797.

Barmouth *above*

The view due west from the small village of Penmaenpool takes in the broad sweep of the estuary of the river Mawddach. Penmaenpool has grown up at a bridging point over the river. Downstream, the Mawddach enters Cardigan Bay close to the exquisite seaside resort of Barmouth. In his account of walking trips in Wales, the poet William Wordsworth summed up Barmouth's attractions: "With a fine sea view in front, the mountains behind, the glorious estuary running eight miles inland, and Cadair Idris within compass of a day's walk, Barmouth can always hold its own against any rival". Notable buildings in the town include Ty Gwyn – a medieval tower house and the 18th-century Ty Crwn prison. There is also a new Lifeboat Visitor Centre.

New Quay *left*

Situated 20 miles south of Aberystwyth on Cardigan Bay, summer visitors to New Quay gaze across the harbour. Such tranquillity was not always possible to find here. In the 18th century the town had a reputation for smuggling and shipbuilding. Its importance as a port increased in the 19th century with the construction of a deeper harbour in the 1830s. As New Quay's shipbuilding declined so the railway link in 1867 brought new opportunities with an increasing flow of visitors. Today New Quay is still a busy place in summer but quiet out of season. The town has a Dylan Thomas connection – in 1944 he lived in a house called "Majoda" above the clifftops and a special trail takes visitors to many of his favourite haunts.

Harlech *above*

The high ground to the east of Harlech provides tremendous views due west over the castle and out across Tremadog Bay. The construction of Harlech Castle began in 1283 during the reign of Edward I. It was one of the "iron ring" fortresses built around the Snowdonia coast to intimidate the Welsh into accepting English rule. Originally, the castle was immediately above the sea, but due to coastal retreat, the stairway called the "way from the sea" no longer descends to a beach. It was an important Lancastrian stronghold during the Wars of the Roses and the song *Men of Harlech* commemorates the garrison's seven-year defence of the castle between 1461-1468.

Borth *left*

The sun sets across the extensive sands at Borth in Ceredigion. The area around the town was once marsh, but it has since been reclaimed. The landscape is marked by dykes and the Afon Leri – a canal built in the 19th century to divert water into the river Dyfi. On the beach are centuries-old tree remains which can be seen when the tide is out.

89

Dinas Dinlle *right*

The magnificent beach at Dinas Dinlle has a foreshore made up of natural pebble banks; this view is looking north-east towards Anglesey. The mountainous headland in the distance is the Twr Mawr lighthouse peninsula on Llanddwyn Island – the location also of an ancient church dedicated to Saint Llanddwyn, the Welsh patron saint of lovers. The cliff above the beach is the site of a much eroded Iron Age hill fort. Roman artefacts found locally bear witness to the area's strategic importance in the 2nd and 3rd centuries.

Fairbourne *below*

This photograph shows *Beddgelert* – a half-size steam train – hard at work on the Fairbourne to Barmouth steam railway that runs between the two towns along the north-west coast of Wales overlooking Cardigan Bay. The train is shown here chugging across the flats just before entering Fairbourne with the bridge (also a part of the route) across the Barmouth estuary in the background. The railway has been in existence since 1895, although the tracks were re-gauged in 1984 to carry its complement of four smaller engines.

Portmeirion *above*

The Italianate village of Portmeirion owes its existence to the architect Sir Clough Williams-Ellis (1883-1978) who built the village on his own private peninsula on the coast of Snowdonia. Construction took 50 years, and many of the buildings incorporate important architectural features which Williams-Ellis rescued from buildings that were being demolished elsewhere. The extensive grounds are criss-crossed with beautiful woodland walks. The main white building in the photograph is the hotel, which dates from 1850; in the distance is the Observatory Tower, designed in 1935. The 1960s television series *The Prisoner* was shot on location at Portmeirion. Today it is a place of pilgrimage for Prisoner fans and tourists alike.

Criccieth Castle *left*

The view due west captures sunset behind Criccieth Castle on its headland jutting into Tremadog Bay. Construction began in the early 13th century at the command of Llywelyn ap Iorwerth, and was later continued by his grandson Llywelyn ap Gruffydd. It was a key stronghold in the wars between England and Wales and was eventually captured by Edward I during his second campaign in north Wales (1282-1283). More recently Criccieth featured in several paintings by Turner depicting shipwrecked mariners.

91

Llanddwyn Island *left*

This small island off the west coast of Anglesey is attached to the mainland at all but very high tides. From the island there are excellent views of Snowdon and the Lleyn Peninsula. A beacon, the Twr Bach (in English, the small tower) was erected to protect shipping and in 1845 a more effective lighthouse, Twr Mawr, shown on the left, was built. Some of the cottages built near the lighthouse as homes for pilots who guided ships up the Menai Strait have been restored in period style and house exhibits about life on the island. Llanddwyn can be reached on foot along the beach from the main Newborough Warren car park on Anglesey. The beautiful beach at Newborough is considered by many to be one of the best in north-west Wales.

Porth Cwyfan

The 13th-century chapel of St Cwyfan perches on the island of Cribina, on the south-west coast of Anglesey. Known as the Church in the Sea, or by its Welsh name of Cwyfan, the chapel has been awarded a grant by Welsh Heritage to repair the roof, walls and windows and to limewash the interior. Elements of the chapel's 12th-century structure still survive, but most of it dates from the 14th century. It is still used for services and is a popular site for weddings.

South Stack Lighthouse

The South Stack lighthouse is situated on Holy Island on the north-west coast of Anglesey. It is considered to be one of the most magnificent lighthouses in Wales. Built in 1809, it has over 400 stone steps which lead down to the island where there is a superb view of the cliff face and the 4,000 pairs of seabirds nesting there during the summer. The Stack is reached via an aluminium bridge – far safer than the original basket and pulley system that transported lighthousemen in earlier years. Designed by Daniel Alexander, the beam of the lighthouse can be seen by ships 28 miles out to sea.

Britannia Bridge *above*

The second bridge to span the Menai Strait was the Britannia Bridge, built by Robert Stephenson, the son of George Stephenson, the pioneer of the railways. Appropriately this bridge was built because the earlier bridge, Thomas Telford's Menai Suspension Bridge, which opened in 1826, had become so busy that a second crossing was required. The tubular rail bridge was completed in 1850 but completely rebuilt in 1970, after the original was destroyed by fire. The replacement bridge has two levels, the lower for the railway line and the upper for the A55 road. The bridge is named after the Britannia Rock, which supports the masonry pier at its centre.

Rhoscolyn *left*

This is the view across to Rhoscolyn Head from Porth Saint beach on the west coast of Anglesey. Rhoscolyn Head lies on the Anglesey Coastal Path which was opened in 2003 and combines existing public footpaths with new routes where the owners have given permission for walking. For over 95 per cent of its length the Coastal Path travels through areas of outstanding natural beauty.

Caernarfon Castle *above*

It took more than 50 years to construct Caernarfon castle. The main period of work began in 1283 and went on until 1323. This formidable building was part of the post-war settlement of north Wales following Edward I's successful campaign against the forces of Llywelyn ap Gruffydd in 1277. Its construction cost £22,000 – an enormous sum at the time, equivalent to more than a year's income for the royal treasury. The castle, designed by the royal architect James St George, was said to have been inspired by the walls of Constantinople – something that prominent crusader Edward I would have appreciated. The tradition of naming the heir to the English throne the Prince of Wales originated here when Edward I offered the Welsh a successor who did not speak a word of English, only to reveal he meant his baby son Edward to inherit his powers in Wales. In the 20th century both Edward VIII and Prince Charles were "invested" with the title "Prince of Wales" at Caernarfon; 4,000 guests attended Prince Charles' investiture in 1969 and a television audience of 500m viewers watched the event, which brought Caernarfon Castle worldwide fame.

Beaumaris Castle *left*

Located in Anglesey opposite the town of Bangor, Beaumaris Castle was another of the stupendous chain of strongholds thrown up along the Snowdonia coastline in order to impose English rule on the Welsh. The building of Beaumaris began in 1295 to a concentric plan by James St George. The castle has a tidal dock which allowed it to be supplied directly from the sea and it was surrounded by an 18ft-wide water-filled moat. The defences include numerous cleverly sited arrow slits. Any enemy besieging Beaumaris would have to overcome 14 separate obstacles and four lines of fortifications, thanks to the "walls within walls" design.

Conwy *left and above*

Conwy is one of Europe's finest examples of a medieval walled town. Conwy castle was built by Edward I between 1283 to 1289 and, together with the castles and walls of Harlech, Caernarfon and Beaumaris, is a World Heritage Site. An estimated £15,000 was spent building the castle and the town's defences. Another of Conwy's tourist attractions is the 1826 Conwy Suspension Bridge built by Thomas Telford over the river Conwy next to the castle. It is claimed that the marshy ground at Conwy Morfa nearby is the place that golf was first played in Wales. It was also where Hugh Iorys Hughes developed and later built the famous floating Mulberry Harbour, used in the invasion of Europe in the Second World War.

Llandudno *right*

Llandudno is a seaside resort on the coast between Bangor and Colwyn Bay, specifically built as a mid-Victorian planned holiday destination. Seen here at sunset is the town's beautiful award-winning pier, which is Grade II listed. Built in 1878, at 2,295ft it is the longest pier in Wales and the fifth longest in England and Wales; when it was built, paddle steamers from Liverpool and the Isle of Man brought visitors to swell the holiday trade. Views out to sea from the pier are magnificent while, on clear days, visitors are rewarded with a view inland across Conwy Bay to the mountains of Snowdonia.

Great Orme *left*

The Great Orme is a limestone headland on the north coast of Wales situated on Llandudno Bay. Magnificent views of Snowdonia and its sister headland, Little Orme, can be enjoyed from the summit which is criss-crossed with paths and is a nature reserve. The best way to reach the top is by taking the tram – Britain's only remaining cable-operated tramway which opened in 1902. The area is famous for its natural wells and a number of these are still supplying water. It is also an area famed for its copper which has been excavated here since the Bronze Age. It is possible to try your hand at copper mining as part of a local tourist activity.

Prestatyn *right*

The seaside resort of Prestatyn, with its magnificent sandy beach, nestles below the steeply wooded slopes and limestone outcrops of Prestatyn Hillside at the northern end of the Clwydian Hills; this stunning landscape is now part of an area of outstanding natural beauty. The town's sheltered position and golden sands, together with the fact that it is the most easterly resort on the north Wales coast, meant that it developed rapidly in the 19th and early 20th centuries. It is at the northern end of the Offa's Dyke Path, the challenging 168-mile walk along the Welsh Borders which starts at Chepstow.

Colwyn Bay *left*

Night-time in Colwyn Bay and the resort lights shine like a string of pearls along the front. The town is situated between Llandudno and Rhyl, while the great sweep of the bay extends from Rhos-on-Sea to Old Colwyn. Its beautiful sandy beaches are ideal for family holidays and swimming, and several have won Blue Flag awards. Sadly, the Victoria pier closed to the public in 1991, after 91 years as one of the town's main attractions. One of the unanswered mysteries is whether the murals decorating the main café by artist Eric Ravilious have survived – they may still exist beneath layers of paint and cladding. Other elements of the pier did not, including the Art Deco pavilion. The pier at Rhos-on-Sea was demolished after storm damage in the 1950s.

North-West England

The north-west coast of England takes in the bright lights of Blackpool, the beautifully restored Merseyside docks, the open sands of Cumbria and the rocky coastline of the Isle of Man with its lighthouses and haunted castles. On this coast the Romans posted garrisons, smugglers and wreckers carried out their dubious trades and racehorses have thundered up and down the sands at Southport in training for the Grand National.

New Brighton *above* and Caldy Beach *right*

The view looking north-east across the sands of New Brighton – with the breakwater and Perch Rock lighthouse in view. The line of docks at Bootle can just be seen in the far distance. The 19th century saw New Brighton's transition from a place with a reputation for smuggling and wrecking to one that promised fun and relaxation for holidaymakers. At Caldy Island (right) on the Wirral coast, the groynes loom like strange sentinels. Beyond them, to the west, is a view of the mountains of north Wales across the river Dee.

The Mersey from New Brighton *above left* and Liverpool Docks *above*

There is no better way to experience Liverpool and Merseyside than from the deck of the famous Mersey ferry. In the 19th century Liverpool became known as the "second port of the Empire" after London, but it suffered badly from the post-war economic decline. Its fortunes have improved in recent years and since 1995 Liverpool has experienced quite startling growth, including the complete overhaul of its waterfront which was declared a World Heritage Site in 2004. Here the view east shows the bronze domes of the Royal Liver Building which, together with the Cunard and Port of Liverpool buildings, form the "Three Graces" of the city's skyline. In addition to the Three Graces Liverpool has over 2,500 other listed buildings including two cathedrals. The Anglican Cathedral Church of Christ in Liverpool is situated close to the modern Roman Catholic Liverpool Metropolitan Cathedral in the city centre.

Southport *below and below right*

Although the elegant resort of Southport has existed as a settlement for centuries, its most rapid period of growth was during Queen Victoria's reign when it gained a reputation as a more sedate resort than Blackpool, its neighbour just up the coast. Among its most famous attractions is the pier – the first ever built purely for recreation in Britain, and its seven miles of golden sands. As well as attracting the holiday crowds, the beaches around Southport have been used to stage attempts to break the land-speed record and they also provided the landing and taking-off points for early transatlantic flights. The sands are popular with horse-racing stables and Birkdale Sands (below) was used for the training gallops of Red Rum, the famous horse which won the Grand National three times.

Blackpool *left and below*

The UK's premier seaside resort, Blackpool's name is probably derived from the black peaty water which flowed into the Irish Sea across an area of marsh at this point on the coast. The town's fortunes are inextricably linked to tourism and most of its sites are associated with it, including the famous Blackpool Tower built in 1894. If it seems familiar then it should – this familiar landmark is a scaled-down replica of the Eiffel Tower. Another much photographed attraction are the double-decker "balloon buses" that ply the promenade. Blackpool has traditionally been the resort of choice for Lancashire city-dwellers and also with Glaswegians. The resort has three piers and the Blackpool Pleasure Beach amusement park, founded in 1896, with rollercoaster rides and family entertainments. There are seven miles of glorious sandy beaches for holidaymakers to enjoy – one of the great traditions for children is a donkey ride up and down the golden sands.

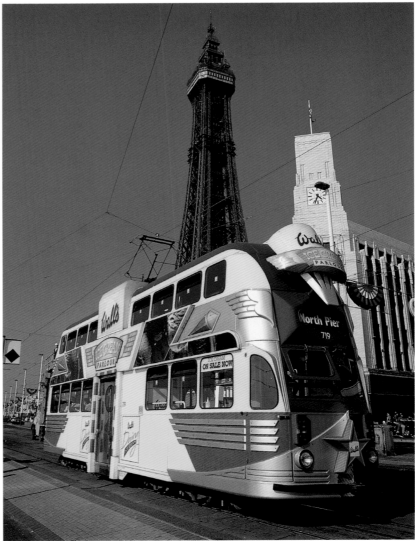

Grange-over-Sands *above*

The view south-west from the Cumbrian resort of Grange-over-Sands looks across Morecambe Bay to the hills of Lancashire in the distance. Once the river Kent used to pass the town but it has, in recent times, changed course to run closer to the Arnside bank of the estuary, leaving the Grange-over-Sand's side dominated by sometimes hazardous mudflats and grass meadows.

St Bees Head *below*

St Bees Head is the westernmost part of the Lake District. It is a site of beauty for walkers – its four-mile clifftop path is the start of the route of the 190-mile coast-to-coast walk. This is a dangerous place for shipping – the rusting hulks of long-forgotten ships lie half-buried in the shingle at the foot of the 300ft (90m) cliffs, which are a haven for many species of seabird.

Ravenglass *above*

The view south-east from Saltcoats on the Cumbrian coast shows Ravenglass spread out along the estuary created by the confluence of three local rivers – the Esk, Mite and Irt. Known as *Glannaventa* to the Romans, this was an important garrison site for over 300 years – although the only substantial local survival from that era is the bath house now known as Walls Castle. Today Ravenglass is the only seaside town within the boundary of the Lake District National Park.

Ulverston *right*

The southern Lakeland market town of Ulverston lies on the Furness peninsula just north of Morecambe Bay and adjacent to Cartmel Sands. The town is mentioned in the Domesday Book and acquired its first market charter in 1280. Today Ulverston calls itself the "Festival Town", a reference to the many themed festivals it hosts each year. Among the most famous is the Lantern Festival, which involves hundreds of Ulverstonians creating lanterns out of willow and tissue paper and parading them through the town centre.

Whitehaven
above

The view is from Whitehaven's north pier looking into the heart of the harbour and marina. In the early 18th century Whitehaven was among the country's top ports, particularly associated with the coal trade. The emergence of Bristol and Liverpool put paid to this prominence. The town has had a colourful history, including a period as a smugglers' haven and it was bombarded from the sea in 1778 during the American War of Independence. Today it has strong commercial links with the nuclear power station at Sellafield.

Douglas *below*

Seen here from the south, from a vantage point above the port on Douglas Head, Douglas has been the capital of the Isle of Man since 1863 (formally that honour belonged to Castletown to the south) and it is home to the Manx Parliament. It has less respectable origins, having a fearsome reputation as a smugglers' haven in the 18th and early 19th centuries and a refuge for English debtors, who were able to escape their mainland creditors by settling here.

Douglas Head *above*

Stop on the Marine Drive south of Douglas, the capital of the Isle of Man, and look north and this is the vista along the coast culminating in the rocky outcrop of Douglas Head. Just around the headland is Douglas Head Lighthouse, which was first established in 1857. Its engineers were David and Thomas Stevenson (father to Robert Louis Stevenson). Its beam flashes out every 10 seconds and has a nominal range of 24 miles. It was automated in 1984.

Calf of Man *right*

Journey to the end of Spanish Head at the most south-westerly point of the Isle of Man and a small island becomes visible across a short stretch of water called Calf Sound. This is the Calf of Man. Nothing to do with young cattle, the name derives from an old Norse word *kalfr* meaning "a small island near a large one". The Calf of Man is home to a large breeding population of Manx shearwaters, a seabird which derives its name from its presence in Man.

Peel *above and* PeelCastle *right*

Linked by a causeway to Peel, Peel Castle stands on tiny St Patrick's Island. It was built in the 11th century by the Vikings, in the reign of King Magnus Barelegs. Today the castle is owned by Manx National Heritage and is open to visitors. Like many other buildings in the town, it is built of red standstone, giving rise to Peel being called "the rose city" because of the gorgeous hues that play on the stone in sunlight. Peel is also the location for the island's only cathedral – St German's. Completed in 1884, its diocese not only includes the islands of Sodor and Man, but also the Hebridean islands off the west coast of Scotland.

Northern Ireland

The Antrim coast road of Northern Ireland is said to be one of the most scenic routes in the British Isles; inaccessible for years, when the coast road was built visitors flocked in droves, the highlight being the natural phenomenon of the Giant's Causeway. For much of its length the coast is flanked with towering cliffs, intersected with villages, waterfalls and the famous Glens of Antrim, beautiful wooded valleys which penetrate inland. From much of this coast the Mull of Kintyre and the islands of Scotland are visible – this is the narrowest strait in the British Isles and the geography bears testimony to the intertwined history of the two countries.

Giant's Causeway *above and right*

Located north of the town of Bushmills on the Antrim coast, the Giant's Causeway is an area of 40,000 interlocking basalt columns resulting from volcanic activity over 60 million years ago. The legend associated with this dramatic spot attributes the site to the giant Fionn mac Cumhail who built it to walk to Scotland in order to smite a Scottish giant called Benandonner. The same eruptions that created the Causeway are responsible for the geology of Fingal's Cave in Scotland. The Causeway is a World Heritage Site and was recently voted the fourth greatest natural wonder in the British Isles.

Ballintoy Church and Rathlin Island *below*

Ballintoy is a small fishing village on the Antrim coast. Among its best-known attractions is the church above the harbour – shown here with its seaward view and Rathlin Island in the distance. Founded in 1560, the church has a colourful history, and lost its steeple during a hurricane in December 1894. It contains some interesting stained glass and memorials including one to David Elder Jamieson who died aboard *HMS Defence* during the battle of Jutland in 1916. Just two fields away from the church is the site of a "famine mass grave" for those who died in 1845-49 during "The Great Hunger", the name given to the Irish potato famine.

Dunluce Castle *above*

On the Antrim coast between Portballintrae and Portrush, Dunluce is one of the most dramatic medieval ruined castles in Ireland. Dunluce transferred from English to Irish ownership in 1584 when it became the stronghold of the MacDonnell clan – the eventual Earls of Antrim. They improved the castle using the proceeds from the sale of goods seized from a Spanish ship (part of the Armada) wrecked nearby. After the Battle of the Boyne in 1690 the MacDonnells were unable to maintain the castle and it steadily became a ruin with much of its stone removed for nearby construction.

Devenish Island *right*

The view over Devenish Island in lower Lough Erne, County Fermanagh, famous for its 6th-century monastery. Among the surviving buildings on Devenish Island are a church, an oratory and a tower – all dating from the 12th century. There is also a 15th-century abbey.

Carrickfergus Castle *below*

The history of Carrickfergus Castle on the shores of Belfast Lough has been particularly violent. Initially, it was home to Norman opportunists such as John de Courcy (who built it in 1177) and Hugh de Lacy – both of whom ruled as petty-kings over huge fiefdoms in Ulster. Carrickfergus was successfully besieged in 1210 by the English King John who placed constables in charge, one of whom, De Serlane, was paid £100 to build new defences. The castle became one of the few reliable English strongholds in Ireland as English power declined in the 16th century. In 1760 it was captured in a French raid. During the Napoleonic Wars it served as a prison and continued to be garrisoned up until 1928. In the Second World War it was used as an air raid shelter and is now a key tourist attraction with a banqueting hall and other exhibits.

Belfast *left*

Opened in 1997, the Waterfront Hall on the banks of the river Lagan is one of Belfast's most recent and widely acclaimed buildings. It cost £32m and took more than three years to build. Its roof is made of bronze and will slowly turn green to mirror the dome of City Hall. Belfast is the second largest city on the island of Ireland after Dublin. Its name derives from the Irish for "mouth of the Farset" – *Béal Feirste* – which is anachronistic given that the river Farset has long since been superseded by the river Lagan as the City's principal waterway. Belfast's history dates back to the Bronze Age, but it became a thriving commercial centre between the 18th and 20th centuries, a centre for linen and rope-making, the tobacco trade and also shipbuilding. It has been the capital of Northern Ireland since 1921. Its recent past has been marred by sectarian conflict between its highly segregated Protestant and Catholic communities. In recent years the violence has diminished as the country attempts to find political solutions to its problems, and its new confidence is reflected in buildings such as the Waterfront Hall.

Carrick-a-Rede *left*

A woman pauses before taking the first step over the 8oft (24m) deep chasm between Carrick Island and the mainland of County Antrim. The rope bridge she must venture across was first placed here by fishermen to inspect their salmon nets. The bridge is now open to anyone walking the coastal path. Once they reach the predominantly limestone Carrick Island, visitors are rewarded with fine views of the Scottish islands and also the many seabirds that use the cliffs here for nesting and sanctuary.

Portbradden *below*

As well as spectacular cliffs and glens, the route along the Antrim coast road brings the traveller to many picturesque seaside villages including Portbradden, with its little harbour, seen here across the sands of Whitepark Bay. Portbradden means the "port of salmon" and there is a salmon fishery nearby. The village is also home to St Gobban's, which claims to be the smallest church in Ireland.

Bangor *left*

The seaside resort of Bangor lies on the southern side of Belfast Lough in County Down. It is the third largest settlement in Northern Ireland and is today principally a commuter town for Belfast. The coming of the railways in 1865 turned Bangor into a fashionable resort. Many of the finest houses in the town date from this period, especially those overlooking the harbour.

Scotland

From the border north of Berwick in the east, to the pretty village of Portpatrick in the west, the Scottish coast is stunning in the variety of its landscape. Rocky outcrops are dotted with magnificent castles, while the rugged coastline provided natural harbours where fishing villages could develop. The Orkneys, Shetlands and the Western Isles are full of varied coastal scenery – stacks, arches, towering sea cliffs and sandy beaches and dunes all providing a wonderful natural habitat for birds and plants. But Scotland's coast is also the site of many beautiful towns – from the home of golf at St Andrews to splendid west coast resorts such as Oban and Portree, this is a coastline rich in history and full of interest for the visitor.

Tantallon Castle *right*

This stronghold was once the first major obstacle any army venturing across Scotland's easternmost border would have encountered. Tantallon Castle is just three miles from North Berwick and its vantage on top of a high cliff gives it an unimpeded view of the Bass Rock in the Firth of Forth. Built in 1358, Tantallon's fortunes finally declined in 1651 when Cromwell destroyed it while rooting out bandits who had been using it as a base.

Forth Bridges *above*

In the foreground is the mammoth structure of the Forth Rail Bridge, built between 1883-1890 to connect Edinburgh and Fife. Regarded as an engineering marvel, it was constructed at some cost to human life. Of the 4,600 people employed to build it, 63 people are thought to have died and hundreds of others were injured. In the distance are the sleek lines of the Forth Road Bridge, built in 1964. When opened, it was the largest suspension bridge in the world and together with the approach viaducts it is over one and a half miles long. The main towers extend 512ft (156m) above the river and the sag of the cables between the towers is approximately 300ft (91m).

St Abb's Head *above and left*

The rocky outcrop and harbour of St Abb's Head in Berwickshire is the point at which the British coastline takes a sharp turn to the left and heads west into the Firth of Forth – until this point it had generally headed north. It was the sinking of a ship called the *Martello* in 1857 that prompted the building of the lighthouse here in 1862. The engineers were David and Thomas Stevenson, who also built the lighthouse at Douglas Head, on the Isle of Man. The beautiful cliffs around St Abb's are a nature reserve and support large colonies of breeding kittiwakes, fulmars, guillemots, razorbills, shags and puffins; the deep waters below are home to a variety of marine life.

111

Bass Rock *above*

One of the world's best examples of a volcanic plug, the Bass Rock rises about 100ft (30m) out of the Firth of Forth. Some 40,000 pairs of gannets shelter and nest here, and from the coast the rock appears white thanks to their guano and their characteristic markings. The castle on Bass Rock was built by the Lauder family in the 15th century, who lost it during the Civil War.

Elie *below*

It may look like the ancient remains of an abbey or castle but the structure overlooking the magnificent vista at Elie in Fife is actually an 18th-century folly. The Lady's Tower was built to serve as a dressing room for a Lady Anstruther, an early naturist, who used to bathe naked in pools nearby while a servant tolled a bell to warn locals to keep away.

Pittenweem *above*

This pretty seaside village is viewed here from the outer harbour wall close to an assortment of lobster and crab traps. Pittenweem's name derives from the Scottish Gaelic and is thought to mean "the place of the cave". The cave in question is probably nearby St Fillan's cave, although there are many other candidates along this indented shoreline. St Fillan is said to have converted the local Pictish population from his cave in the 8th century. The cave was rediscovered around 1900 when a horse ploughing in the priory garden stumbled down into it. The white village houses with red roofs shown in the photograph illustrate the classic East Neuk of Fife building style, influenced by trade with the Low Countries of Belgium and the Netherlands. Many of the historic buildings in the village have been restored by the Scottish National Trust.

Crail *right*

The most easterly of Fife's fishing ports, this tranquil village was first granted its royal charter by Robert the Bruce in 1310. Crail harbour is one of the oldest and the best in the area and there was trading with the Continent as far back as the 9th century. Traces of this link can be seen in the town's architecture, some of which has a Dutch influence and in the town's medieval marketplace – one of the largest in Europe.

St Andrews *below*

Despite being named after the apostle Saint Andrew, the first holy figure associated with this site is Kenneth, who established a monastery here in the 6th century. Today, St Andrews is host to Scotland's oldest university and also enjoys an international reputation as the "home of golf". It is here that The Royal and Ancient Golf Club has its headquarters – one of the oldest and most beautiful courses in the world and the frequent location of the Open Championship, the oldest of the four big golf competitions held annually. The view is of the ruins of the Cathedral of St Andrew, once one of Scotland's largest buildings.

Stonehaven *above*

Situated on the coast south of Aberdeen, there has been a settlement at Stonehaven since Neolithic times. A popular resort and fishing village, its harbour was part-designed by Robert Louis Stevenson's grandfather. It has major cultural associations – in the early 19th century it was a holiday retreat for the great Scottish poet Robert Burns; in 1899 John Reith was born there, the founder of the BBC and later to become Lord Reith of Stonehaven. The town's major tourist attraction apart from the nearby beaches is Dunnottar Castle (opposite).

Dundee *left*

The prow of the *Unicorn* – a 46-gun frigate built in 1824 – frames this photograph of Dundee while in the background stands Scott's *Discovery*. Both ships are testament to the long history of shipbuilding here on the north bank of the Tay. Dundee is known as the place of "jam, jute and journalism" thanks to its other historic industries.

Fraserburgh *above*

Forty miles north-east of Aberdeen, the beautiful beach at Fraserburgh is popular with walkers and holidaymakers. The Fraser family bought up much of the surrounding area in the late 16th century and their castle was converted into Scotland's first mainland lighthouse in 1787, renamed Kinnaird Head Lighthouse.

Dunnottar Castle *left*

The ruins of the medieval fortress of Dunnottar Castle, near Stonehaven, stand guard over the sea. This was home to the Keith clan and was used as a secure place in times of strife for the Scottish crown jewels. The ruins are spread over a three acre area virtually surrounded by 160ft (50m) high sheer cliffs. In 1990 Dunnottar was used as the key location in the Mel Gibson and Glenn Close screen version of *Hamlet*.

Aberdeen South Pier *below*

A massive wave crashes into Aberdeen's South Pier, driven on by the prevailing winds. The 1,050ft (320m) breakwater with the Girdleness Lighthouse (built 1833) are both almost entirely obscured by the spray on such days. Aberdeen harbour, designed by John Smeaton and Thomas Telford, is a triumph of civil engineering. The city's docks are as important as they have ever been, playing a crucial role in the supply and support of the North Sea oilfields. Aberdeen is the principal commercial port in northern Scotland and an international port for general cargo and container traffic.

Cruden Bay *below*

The romantic Dunbury rock arch sits just off the Aberdeenshire coast near the village of Cruden Bay. In 1012 the settlement was the site of a battle between the Scots and invading Scandinavian raiders; it is thought that its name derives from the Gaelic for "slaughter of Danes". Today, Cruden Bay attracts tourists with its hotels and golf course.

Duncansby Head *right*

Near the inland village of John O'Groats, Duncansby Head, with its remarkable stacks is the most northerly spot on the north-east coast of Scotland. The Stacks of Duncansby and Thirle Door Arch are truly dramatic – especially with the air around them filled with the movement and sound of the large colonies of seabirds here. Duncansby Head is also the site of a lighthouse built in 1924. This beautiful stretch of coastline is reached via a single-track road from John O'Groats; on arrival, visitors are rewarded with views north over Orkney and west to Dunnet Head, the most northerly point on mainland Britain. A short walk behind the lighthouse and the view opens up to the south, over the Stacks and the Arch.

Orkney *above and above right*

Situated approximately 10 miles north of the Caithness coast, the Orkneys are a group of around 70 islands containing some of the most dramatic cliffs and rock formations in Britain. Mainland is the largest of the group, followed by Hoy; this photograph is of Hoy glimpsed through the mist from Mainland. The Old Man of Hoy is a sandstone rock stack rising from the sea to a height of 450ft (137m) off the west coast of Hoy and is considered a classic challenge by rock climbers.

The first successful ascent was televised in 1966. Modern techniques and equipment, however, have made it more accessible to slightly less experienced climbers and it has now been conquered many times. The Old Man of Hoy's days may be numbered as it takes a terrific beating from the sea and prevailing wind each winter. Eventually, like all such stacks it can be expected to crumble and fall into the surrounding sea.

Skara Brae *left*

The photograph suggests something of the extraordinary scale of this Neolithic village, located on the west coast of Mainland. Skara Brae, which has been designated as a World Heritage Site, lay hidden for thousands of years until a great storm in 1850 blew away the sand and grass that had enveloped it. Early excavation up until 1868 revealed the remains of four ancient buildings. Further work in the 1920s and 30s uncovered the rest of the village – which comprises some eight dwellings. Carbon dating in the early 1970s revealed that the settlement had been occupied between 3200 and 2500BC, when it was abandoned, possibly because of the colder climate.

Eshaness *below*

The most northerly part of Britain, Shetland is an
archipelago made up of more than one hundred islands. It
was Norse until 1468, when it was sold to Scotland for 8,000
florins as a part of the royal marriage settlement between
James III of Scotland and Princess Margrethe of Denmark.
The district of Eshaness at the western tip of Northmavine
contains some of the most spectacular sites in all Shetland.
Here giant Atlantic rollers smash into black cliffs and the sea
has carved a set of precipitous stacks – most notably the
Drongs and Dore Holm, an awesome natural arch. The
lighthouse at Eshaness has been automated since 1974;
together with two other lighthouses on Shetland it is
available to rent as a holiday property.

Ullapool *left and right*

Two views of Ullapool, the beautiful west coast fishing village and resort. The town is situated on the eastern shore of Loch Broom (left); further along that same shore lies the port of Ullapool, a centre of herring fishing following its founding in 1788. Its harbour was designed by Thomas Telford and is still in use today as a yachting haven and ferry port for traffic to the Outer Hebrides. Ullapool has a strong reputation as a centre of music and performance, particularly during the summer months.

Arisaig *above*

The silver sands of the glorious beach at Arisaig, to the west of Fort William. The village is a stop on the romantically named "Road to the Isles", and visitors who take this route will be entranced by the views of the islands of Rhum, Eigg and Skye. The remains of ruined cottages throughout this area are a reminder of one of Scotland's darkest hours. In 1801 over 1,000 crofters were cleared off the land to make way for sheep and taken to Nova Scotia as part of the widespread policy of clearances across the Highlands.

Plockton *above*

Looking due north over the seaward end of Loch Carron on the north-west coast of Scotland to the pretty village of Plockton. This was a planned village established in the 18th century in an attempt to stem the flood of Scottish emigration. The village is a popular tourist resort, especially since it was chosen as the location of the television series *Hamish Macbeth*. Nearby is Duncraig Castle, a 19th-century stately home built by the Matheson family.

Kyle of Lochalsh *left*

The most prominent building in Kyle is the Lochalsh Hotel with its slipway; until 1995 visitors could catch ferries here to the Isle of Skye before a bridge was built. The village received the greatest boost to its prosperity first with a road from Inverness in 1819 and then the coming of the railway in 1897.

Old Man of Storr *right*

There are few more famous spots in western Scotland than the Storr – a rocky hill on the Trotternish peninsula overlooking the Sound of Raasay. The hill consists of a number of wonderfully shaped pinnacles or volcanic plugs.

Portree *below*

Portree is the main town on Skye. Its name comes from the Gaelic *Port-an-Righ,* or "King's Port" and this dates back to a visit by King James V who arrived with a fleet of ships in 1540 demanding that the island support him. One of the town's most important buildings is the Royal Hotel – the site of Bonnie Prince Charlie's farewell to Flora MacDonald in 1746. He would never see Scotland again. Many other Scots people would leave never to return from Portree – the start of their long haul to America and Canada. Modern Portree offers visitors many attractions including its own immediate picturesque surroundings and the nearby "Lump" – as the peninsula south of the town is called.

Oban *right*

Known as "the Gateway to the Isles" the beautiful resort town of Oban, on the west coast of Scotland, is the principal port for the Western Isles with ferry services to Colonsay, Barra, Tiree and South Uist. Its importance was enhanced in 1880 with the coming of

the railways. The town itself lies in a beautiful setting on Oban Bay and boasts a number of interesting buildings including McCaig's Tower which, like a coronet of stone, contains nothing more than the top of the hill on which it stands. As well as the ferry terminal, Oban is a centre for leisure sailing and is also the starting point of the "coast-to-coast" walk that reaches as far as St Andrews.

South Uist

The standing stone at Pollachar on the south coast of South Uist (the second largest of the Western Isles) stands like a silent watcher over the Sound of Barra with the islands of Eriskay and Barra in the distance. It is a reminder of the ancient Celtic traditions and culture on these islands that still run deep today. Despite its small size – South Uist is only 22 miles north to south and seven miles wide – it enjoys a wide variety of scenery including an almost unbroken stretch of beach on the west coast and substantial mountains in the east which, in the case of Beinn Mhor, rise to 2033ft (620m). South Uist people have endured much persecution thanks to their Catholicism and language (Gaelic) and many were evicted in the 1840s as part of the Highland Clearances – leaving their traditional land to start a new life in Canada.

Eigg and Rhum *right*

This view from the beach at Traigh Chlithe on the Inner Hebridean island of Eigg takes in the Bay of Laigg with the larger island of Rhum on the horizon. Rhum is owned by Scottish Natural Heritage and is considered of worldwide importance thanks to its plant and animal species and the habitats that support them. Among the many bird species that nest here is a colony of over 100,000 Manx shearwaters.

The Cuillins *below*

This photograph across Loch Scavaig shows the Cuillins in all their magnificence. They have been described as the most dramatic range in Britain and are much visited by walkers and climbers; for the less intrepid there are sightseeing boat trips from Elgol.

Harris *above and right*

In Scottish Gaelic Harris – the southern part of the
largest of the Outer Hebridean islands – is known as
Na Hearadh. The northern part of the island is called
Lewis. The photograph is taken on the west coast of
South Harris, the side that faces the North Atlantic
and which is blessed with some of the best beaches in
Scotland. South Harris, as can be seen from this view
(right) across Loch Leosavay, is barren. Among its main
settlements is Rodel with the medieval kirk of St
Clement's. One of the main tourist routes on Harris is
the "Golden Road", which hugs the south-east coast
from Tarbert to Rodel. It is so-named because of the
high cost of its construction through difficult terrain.

Iona Abbey *left*

The Isle of Iona lies just a mile off the western tip of the Isle of Mull. Due to its association with St Columba, who established a monastery here in 563, it has long been a centre of Christianity and pilgrimage. The abbey, which is also the burial place of the early Scottish kings, was originally a medieval Benedictine foundation; today it is one of Scotland's most historic and venerated sites.

Luskentyre *above*

South Harris is famed for its beaches and the largest and arguably the best of them is Luskentyre. It lies near the narrow isthmus that connects North and South Harris. At high tide much of the bay is submerged, becoming part of the Sound of Taransay. Here the breathtaking view shows the island of Taransay in the distance. The fact that few people live locally adds to the appeal of these beaches.

Tobermory Harbour *right*

Tobermory means "Mary's Well" in Gaelic. The capital of the Isle of Mull, it is located on a superb natural harbour, and was developed as a planned fishing town by the British Fisheries Society. Many buildings in Tobermory, particularly shops and restaurants, are painted in assorted bright colours, making it a popular location for television programmes, including the children's show *Balamory*. It is also famous by association with the Wombles – one of whom was named Tobermory.

Dunvaig Castle *right*

Situated on the rugged shores of Islay, Dunvaig Castle was once a major stronghold belonging to the lords Donald. The castle lies on a rocky headland at the east side of Lagavulin Bay, just east of Port Ellen. In the 17th century it was fought over by Alasdair "Old" Colkitto MacDonald, first with the Campbells of Cawdor and then with the Covenanting Army under David Leslie (1601-82). Leslie took the castle following a siege and hanged MacDonald from the walls. The Campbells of Cawdor then occupied the castle until the 1670s when Sir Hugh Campbell demolished it and moved to the more comfortable Islay House nearby.

Isle of Arran *left and right*

This is the seventh largest Scottish island and it lies in the Firth of Clyde. The north of the island is a mountainous place with at least one peak, Goat Fell, reaching above 2,600ft (800m). It has been referred to as "Scotland in miniature" as it is divided into "Highland" and "Lowland" areas. There are many stone circles and standing stones dating from Neolithic times, including the standing stones on Machrie Moor and the Giant's Graves above Whiting Bay. St Columba and St Ninian are said to have stayed on Arran and the King's Cave is reputed to have been used by Robert the Bruce as a refuge.

Isle of Jura *above*

The word *jura* is thought to derive from the Old Norse word for deer. This is appropriate, as Jura today supports a large population of red deer. The photograph shows the car ferry that operates across the Sound of Islay between Islay and Feolin Ferry on Jura. Jura is dominated by three steep-sided conical mountains on its western side – the Paps of Jura which rise to over 2,500ft (762m). Its west coast is home to a number of raised beaches – left high and dry by shifts in the sea level or even uplifted by earthquakes. Jura is associated with a literary earthquake too, as it was here that novelist George Orwell completed his masterpiece *Nineteen Eighty-Four*.

Ailsa Craig *above*

The island of Ailsa Craig is located approximately 10 miles west of Girvan, off the coast of South Ayrshire. Here we see it next to the island of Pladda viewed from Arran. Ailsa Craig was a haven for Roman Catholics during the Scottish Reformation. Ailsa Craig is now uninhabited and its lighthouse has been automated since the 1970s. The island is now an important bird sanctuary. Huge numbers of gannets nest here. Recent efforts to rid the island of rats have made it possible for puffin to again nest here after many years absence.

Portpatrick *left*

The pretty village of Portpatrick appears to cling to the south-westerly tip of mainland Scotland. Its position on the curiously named Rhins of Galloway gives unimpeded views of Ireland across the Irish Channel. The town dates back some 500 years and owes its existence to nearby Dunskey Castle. In the late 19th century it was a key stop for ferries carrying traffic to Ireland but its exposed position and the prevailing westerly winds meant that Stranraer became the pre-eminent ferry port; nevertheless, Portpatrick survived the transition from ferry port to resort and today the village marks the start of the Southern Uplands long-distance footpath.